FACILITY AND EQUIPMENT MANAGEMENT
for SPORTDIRECTORS

John R. Olson, PhD
District Coordinator of Athletics
Madison, Wisconsin, School District

Human Kinetics

Library of Congress Cataloging-in-Publication Data

Facility and equipment management for sportdirectors / John R.
Olson.
  p. cm.
"The sportdirector series is a revolutionary approach to the craft
of managing athletic programs"—P.
Includes index.
ISBN 0-87322-940-1
1. Sports facilities—United States—Management. 2. Sporting
goods—United States—Management. I. Title.
GV429.057 1997
796'.06'8—dc20   96-28490
                                                           CIP

ISBN: 0-87322-940-1

Resources in Appendices A and B are reprinted, by permission, copyright 1995, *Athletic Business Magazine*.

Resources in Appendix C are reprinted, by permission, from L.L. Jannott, 1994, *Architect's Catalog* (Fairfield, CT: Rick Jannott), 245-267.

Acquisitions Editor: Jim Kestner; **Developmental Editor:** Jan Colarusso Seeley; **Assistant Editor:** Lynn M. Hooper; **Editorial Assistant:** Coree Schutter; **Copyeditor:** Judith Gallagher; **Proofreader:** Sarah Wiseman; **Indexer:** Barbara E. Cohen; **Graphic Designer:** Stuart Cartwright; **Graphic Artist:** Yvonne Winsor; **Cover Designer:** Stuart Cartwright; **Author Photo:** Photo Express; **Illustrator:** Patrick Griffin, cartoons, and Stuart Cartwright; **Printer:** Versa Press

Printed in the United States of America

10 9 8 7 6 5 4 3 2 1

Human Kinetics
Web site: http://www.humankinetics.com/

United States: Human Kinetics
P.O. Box 5076
Champaign, IL 61825-5076
1-800-747-4457
e-mail: humank@hkusa.com

Canada: Human Kinetics, Box 24040
Windsor, ON N8Y 4Y9
1-800-465-7301 (in Canada only)
e-mail: humank@hkcanada.com

Europe: Human Kinetics, P.O. Box IW14
Leeds LS16 6TR, United Kingdom
(44) 1132 781708
e-mail: humank@hkeurope.com

Australia: Human Kinetics
57A Price Avenue
Lower Mitcham, South Australia 5062
(08) 277 1555
e-mail: humank@hkaustralia.com

New Zealand: Human Kinetics
P.O. Box 105-231, Auckland 1
(09) 523 3462
e-mail: humank@hknewz.com

This effort is dedicated to my family—to my wife Marlene, for her continuing support; to my children, Laurie, Mike, Kristin, and David, for their love and patience; to the memory of my mother and father, Dorothy and John; and to the memory of my brother and sister-in-law, Bill and Margaret.

Contents

Foreword   ix

Series Preface   x

Acknowledgments   xii

Introduction   xiii

PART I: PLANNING FOR EFFECTIVE FACILITY AND EQUIPMENT MANAGEMENT

Chapter 1: Understanding Your Role as a Facility and Equipment Manager   **3**
Developing Your Personal Philosophy   4
Analyzing Your Personal Philosophy   5
Analyzing Your Organization's Philosophy   5
Personal Versus Organizational Philosophies   8
Philosophical Principles and Facility Planning   10
Recognizing Your Role   11
Recognizing the Roles of Others   13
Establishing Goals and Objectives   15

Chapter 2: Assessing Your Facility and Equipment Needs   **17**
Sizing Up the Organization   17
Determining Equipment and Facility Needs   18
Balancing Needs and Resources   21

Chapter 3: Developing a Facility and Equipment Management Plan   **29**
Attending to Legal Considerations   29
Keeping and Using Records   32
Involving Members of the Organization   34
Planning for Evaluation   34

PART II: IMPLEMENTING AND EVALUATING THE FACILITY AND EQUIPMENT MANAGEMENT PLAN

Chapter 4: Managing Equipment   41
Purchasing Equipment   42
Storing Equipment   46
Distributing Equipment   47
Repairing Equipment   49
Evaluating Your Equipment Management Plan   50

Chapter 5: Managing Facilities: Maintenance   53
Determining Facility Maintenance Responsibilities   54
Determining Timelines   54
Preparing Facilities for Instruction, Practice, and Competition   60
Evaluating Your Facility Maintenance Plan   60
Site-Specific Checklists   60

Chapter 6: Managing Facilities: Supervision   79
Identifying Facilities for Which You Are Responsible   80
Identifying Supervisors   80
Training Supervisors   81
Scheduling Supervisors   82
Determining Policy: Ten Legal Duties   82
Monitoring Supervisors   84
Facility and Equipment Conditions   84
Evaluating Your Supervision Plan   85

Chapter 7: Managing Facilities: Scheduling   91
Identifying Facilities for Which You Are Responsible   92
Determining Facility Needs   92
Institutional Philosophy and Scheduling   93
Nonschool Users and Private Rentals   93
Procedures for Reserving Facilities   94
Scheduling Adapted Sport Activities   96
Equity Considerations   96
Scheduling Activities at Other Sites   97
Evaluating Your Facility Scheduling Plan   97

Chapter 8: Facility Planning   103
Funding Sources   104
Primary Planning Committee   105
Hiring an Architectural and Construction Consultant   106
Construction Site Considerations   108
Request for Proposals: The Bid Process   111
Legal and Legislative Considerations   114
Safety Standards   115
Presenting the Selected Proposal   115
Contract Provisions   116
Evaluating Your Facility Construction Plan   116

Chapter 9: Facility Renovation   **119**

Remodeling: An Attractive Alternative   119
A Renovation Planning Committee   120
Assessing Existing Facilities   120
Feasibility Considerations   120
Political Considerations   121
Economic Considerations   121
Developing the Renovation Proposal   121
Letting Bids   122
Evaluating Your Renovation Plan   122

Appendix A Organizations That Publish Equipment
    and Facility Standards   133

Appendix B Resources for Facility and Equipment Management   138

Appendix C Resources for Planning and Renovating Facilities   139

Index   147

About the Author   152

About ASEP   153-154

Foreword

Those of us who have chosen to be directors of sport programs have a daunting task ahead of us. We are charged with operating multi-million dollar facilities that house high-tech building systems and with managing the sophisticated pieces of exercise equipment that are in such demand today. We are expected to schedule creatively, to maximize the use of activity areas, and to insure that our clientele are satisfied customers. In addition, we need to be visionaries in renovating existing spaces and in seeking new construction to meet the needs of the future.

As the director of a sport program, you will be asked to wear many different hats, from that of a construction coordinator to a purchasing agent, and everything in between. The question is this: Where and how does one acquire the knowledge to perform all these tasks? Preparation begins in the classroom. We continue to learn from our experiences on the job and from sharing our experiences and ideas with colleagues. However, there still needs to be a resource guide for us—a road map that helps give us a sense of direction.

I believe *Facility and Equipment Management for SportDirectors* is that resource guide. It provides and identifies key factors that need to be addressed in the overall scope of sport facility and equipment management. This book details, step by step, answers to the questions that you will face as a facility and equipment director. The advice presented here will lead to enhanced performance in your management role and in those people who work with you. This book will also allow you to draw upon the expertise and successes of others, which can only lead to a more rewarding and self-fulfilling career in sport facility and equipment management.

I've had the good fortune and pleasure of knowing John Olson for the past 15 years, and he is someone who not only has the ability to articulate his thoughts on paper but also is able to bolster these ideas with professional and practical experiences. His many years of service in the interscholastic and collegiate arena have provided him with a wealth of knowledge in sport facility and equipment management and make it natural for him to share his experiences and thoughts in *Facility and Equipment Management for SportDirectors*.

As I've read through this resource guide, I have come away with a number of ways to improve and enhance the recreational facilities operation here at the University of Wisconsin-Madison, and I'm confident you will benefit as well. John Olson's outstanding contribution in facility and equipment management will stand as the benchmark resource guide for sport directors now and into the 21st century.

John G. Paine
Director of Recreational Facilities
University of Wisconsin–Madison

Series Preface

The SportDirector Series is a revolutionary approach to the craft of managing athletic programs. Underlying the resources in this series is a set of principles drawn from a careful examination of the day-to-day responsibilities sport directors face. These principles have been framed as a sequence of tests, which each series resource has been designed to pass:

- Is the resource practical?
- Is it affordable?
- Does it save time?
- Is it easy to use?

- Is it up-to-date?
- Is it flexible enough to meet the needs of different programs?
- Does using one resource from the series make it easier to use others?

To ensure that every resource passes these tests, we have worked closely with an editorial advisory board of prominent, experienced athletic directors from across the nation. With the board's assistance, we have developed the series to enable you to benefit from the latest thinking in directing sport programs. Each resource leads you carefully through three steps: planning, implementing, and evaluating.

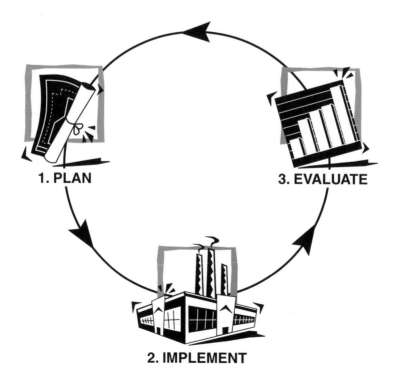

1. PLAN

2. IMPLEMENT

3. EVALUATE

What's so new about the approach? Nothing—until you actually apply it. That's where the series really breaks the mold. Besides telling you how important it is to plan for success in directing your programs, each resource will lead you step-by-step through that planning process. Forms and exercises will help you explore your role and philosophy within the organization, examine your particular needs, and then develop an effective plan of action. In each SportDirector resource these steps are applied specifically to the task at hand. For example, it is essential to assess your needs carefully as you carry out each of your program responsibilities: How you assess promotional needs, however, will differ significantly from how you assess personnel management needs. The series follows the same practical approach to lead you through the implementation and evaluation of your plan.

This approach is possible only because the series authors are experts not only in sport management but also in the specific areas they write about. With the help of the editorial advisory board, these authors translate their knowledge into practical, easy-to-follow recommendations, ready-to-use forms and checklists, and countless practical tips so that you will come away with better ideas for directing your program. The authors also help you take advantage of the latest technology.

New and experienced interscholastic athletic directors alike will find that these resources take into account their widespread responsibilities and limited staff and funding assistance. Directors of Olympic National Governing Body club sport programs and other national and state sport directors will find valuable tools to enhance their efficiency and increase their effectiveness. Students of sport administration will find these resources valuable companions for understanding how to step into the field with confidence to succeed. And all sport directors will find that these tools help them to help the athletes, coaches, parents, and others in their organizational community.

Even more than a leader, you are the architect of your organization's athletic community. As you design and oversee the construction and maintenance of that community, you are in a unique position to ensure that the program achieves a common purpose. The SportDirector Series is conceived not only to help you attend to your everyday duties but also to coalesce your efforts to carry out your program's mission—to make your athletic community the best it can be.

—Jim Kestner

Acknowledgments

Facility and Equipment Management for SportDirectors is a compilation of practical strategies to enhance your leadership and supervisory skills in managing sport facilities and equipment inventories. These contemporary methods, guidelines, and techniques have been drawn from successful experiences and practices. In this regard, I extend personal thanks to John Paine, director of recreation facilities at the University of Wisconsin–Madison, for his contributions, advice, and assistance. In addition, I am indebted to Frank Dropsho, director of building services of the Madison (Wisconsin) Metropolitan School District, for his technical expertise and guidance in my preparing the chapters that discuss new construction and the renovation of sport facilities. To Jan Seeley and Jim Kestner of Human Kinetics, I am particularly thankful for editorial guidance, suggestions, and encouragement throughout the preparation of this work. I cannot adequately thank my secretary, Cindy Plautz, who undertook untold additional responsibilities and extra hours to make this book possible, never losing her consistent, high-level efficiency. And finally, but most importantly, to my wife, Marlene, my sincere thanks for your support and encouragement during this process and throughout the past 38 years.

Introduction

As director or manager of a comprehensive sport facility, you will be responsible for overall programming, operation, maintenance, and enhancement of assets that are among the most heavily used within any community. You will interact with educational and community leaders, classroom instructors, recreation supervisors, athletic coaches, parents, citizen-taxpayers, and students on a regular basis. Each user group will have different needs and interests, but all will expect you to respond quickly and efficiently to their requests.

How well you satisfy the various user groups will result largely from your leadership skills and your ability to make decisions and set priorities. To achieve high-level satisfaction, you will need to assess program effectiveness, participant opinions, facility and equipment conditions, and resource usage patterns on a regular basis.

This book provides an overview of management techniques, strategies, and considerations. In some cases, it will validate procedures that you are using in the management of your facilities or that you see other program supervisors or facility managers using. In other cases, this material will provide new insight and direction for your management efforts. In either case, we are pleased to provide you with modern, field-tested guidelines for the management of comprehensive sport facilities and large equipment inventories.

In part I, the focus is on planning for effective facility and equipment management. The foundation for your planning efforts is your own personal philosophy, which will give direction and consistency to your operational efforts. Chapter 1 explains the importance of defining your philosophy and meshing it with the philosophy of your institutional leadership. To facilitate your efforts, a number of forms and checklists are provided. Use them to articulate your facility management philosophy and to examine those forces that have influenced its development. These practical exercises will also help you to compare and contrast your philosophic ideals, goals, and objectives with those of your institutional leadership.

Chapter 2 describes various resources you can use to assess the needs of your program and the interests of various user groups. It also suggests ways to evaluate the degree to which participants are satisfied by the existing facilities and equipment. It provides forms and checklists for determining how many athletic, instructional, intramural, and recreational participants will require facility access and programming. And it asks you to consider whether your management philosophy is consistent with the needs of each user group that you identify.

Chapter 3 emphasizes important operational components of your facility management plan. It cites legal considerations and the need for focused risk management efforts, accurate record-keeping, and responsive budget planning. It emphasizes evaluation as an ongoing management responsibility.

In part II, specific strategies for implementing and evaluating your plans are discussed in detail. Chapter 4 provides guidelines, checklists, and forms that illustrate important components of an equipment management plan. Topic coverage includes inventory, budgeting, purchasing, storage, distribution, and custody. Computer technology is also discussed; its creative use can enhance your efforts in the areas of inventory control and planning for maintenance, reconditioning, and replacement of equipment.

Chapter 5 describes the importance of facility maintenance to the satisfaction and safety of participants. Staff responsibilities and timelines for in-house and contracted maintenance services are discussed as important components of a long-range, time-sensitive management plan. Accounting for maintenance of facilities used by your athletes or recreation participants but not under your control is also discussed. Forms are provided that will help you correlate the maintenance of equipment and facilities to the needs of various users and to their activity calendars.

Chapter 6 provides operational guidance to you as the overall supervisor and coordinator of the multiple activities that occur within your facility. It suggests ways to schedule activities in appropriate facilities while making use of safe, well-maintained equipment inventories. It also provides program-specific checklists for activity supervisors that will help them to promote maximum enjoyment and satisfaction among their diverse participant populations.

Chapter 7 considers the multiple aspects of facility scheduling by athletic, instructional, recreational, and private-sector users. It discusses philosophic issues, equity considerations, and facility access procedures, along with techniques for scheduling access to facilities that are under the control of other agencies.

Chapter 8 outlines a comprehensive model for planning and conducting new facility construction. It strongly encourages the retention of a professional engineer or architect, who will serve as your liaison to various builders and contractors and as an advocate for the institution and citizen-taxpayers. Various checklists are also provided to facilitate your preconstruction planning efforts and to monitor cost-effectiveness during construction.

Chapter 9 discusses facility renovation as an economical alternative to new construction. It provides guidelines for assessing project feasibility, the political environment, the condition of existing facilities, and the needs of various user groups. It also covers procedures for letting renovation project bids and shows how to monitor the progress of an actual remodeling project.

Finally, the appendixes identify various organizations and planning resources to support your management efforts. These agencies will facilitate your research into innovative methods, techniques, materials, and equipment and will enhance your management of comprehensive sport facilities and equipment inventories.

Part I

Planning for Effective Facility and Equipment Management

*C*hapter *1*

Understanding Your Role as a Facility and Equipment Manager

In your role as a manager or director of one or more sport facilities and numerous equipment inventories, you may often be entrusted to conduct your daily business without direct supervision or immediate guidance from your administrative leaders. Instructors, coaches, and recreation directors are preoccupied with supervision of their sport, recre-ational, or classroom endeavors, while senior organizational leaders are focused on the larger task of operating a school or college.

Although they may not seem interested in your work, all user groups and organizational leaders expect high-level operational efficiency and customer responsiveness in your management of buildings, outdoor sites, supplies, and equipment. To meet their needs, you will need to draw on a set of philosophical ideals and principles to guide you in your daily management procedures. In fact, development of these values is the foundation for success in the field of facility and equipment management.

The first step is to define and analyze your beliefs and personal values concerning the management tasks and responsibilities you have been assigned. Of equal importance is the need to compare your personal management beliefs to the organizational values that may have evolved through tradition or that are important to the leadership of your organization. Take time to commit your personal philosophy of facility and equipment management to paper. You will benefit from the activity and will be enlightened by the comparisons. The practical importance of congruence between your management philosophy and that of your institutional leadership will be discussed throughout this chapter.

In this chapter, you will learn

1. the importance of organizational and personal philosophies as foundations for the task of equipment and facility management,

2. the role of a facility manager in defining and implementing a philosophy,

3. the roles of others in your facility and equipment management plan,

4. the importance of setting specific goals and objectives as tangible components of a management philosophy, and

5. methods for defining program goals and objectives.

DEVELOPING YOUR PERSONAL PHILOSOPHY

Managing highly diverse indoor and outdoor sport facilities and comprehensive equipment inventories is a challenging task that requires program managers

and activity supervisors to engage in careful, ongoing assessment and planning efforts. You should be able to determine priorities and implement focused management strategies aimed at customer satisfaction and efficient operations. Because sport and recreation facilities often serve large and diverse user groups, it is important that your philosophy be clearly linked to the needs and interests of your customers and give direction to responsive planning and strategy development. This philosophical base must also give direction to a range of management practices that are efficient, cost-effective, and financially sound.

Although philosophies are generally expressed as idealized value statements, they must be practical as well. You must always be able to translate them into operational terms that give clear and practical direction to planning, management, and supervision of various activity sites and equipment inventories. The following sample management philosophies illustrate both the practicality and the diversity of this concept within the philosophy statements of seven different activity programs.

1. Facility use will be directed by cost-effective policies and practices that assure maximum access by sports teams, recreation users, and instructional groups. Thus, you may be asked to develop equal access policies for each activity and to purchase equipment that will be shared by all user groups.

2. Facility use will be reserved primarily for campus recreation users, fitness trainers, elective physical education students, and physical education professional majors. This philosophic foundation lets you deny or delay responses to athletic department requests for access to your facilities.

3. Facilities will be jointly and equally available to male and female physical education students and athletes. Equity in the scheduling of all activities should be evident. Moreover, mixed-gender classes should be the norm.

4. Facility use will be equally assigned to the physical education and dance instructional programs, the intramural program, and the interscholastic (intercollegiate) athletic program. In this model, scheduling should be equitable.

5. Equipment acquisition programs will reflect student and faculty recreational and condi-

tioning needs and interests. Participant opinions and attitudes will be assessed regularly.

6. Equipment acquisition programs will reflect student and faculty usage patterns, interest surveys, annual inventories, and equipment conditions. Along with the attitudinal data cited in the preceding philosophy, usage statistics will be important.

7. Equipment acquisition for instructional programs will be funded by state or local fiscal revenues; athletic equipment acquisition will be funded by contest revenues, alumni donations, and other gifts. The athletic department will be asked to make a defined contribution to the tax-supported department budget for annual equipment purchases.

ANALYZING YOUR PERSONAL PHILOSOPHY

As you consider the components of your personal management philosophy, remember that previous experiences and biases may influence your personal perspective. These factors must be carefully considered because of their potential impact on

1. planning efforts involving other supervisors,
2. compatibility with organizational priorities and policies, and
3. your initial success as a facility manager.

Putting It in Writing

It's important to commit your philosophy to paper and review it periodically. This will help you respond to the needs and interests of contemporary user groups through review, comparison, and modification of foundation-level belief statements. Instructional and activity programs tend to reflect the existing philosophy, but regular examination of your personal beliefs can lead you to identify emerging instructional, recreational, intramural, or athletic needs.

Assessing Personal Biases

Although you may have reached agreement with organizational leaders on the key components of a leadership and management philosophy, you must continually monitor the degree to which your operational decisions are free of personal bias. Exercise 1.1 asks you to assess the impact of past experiences on your management decisions.

ANALYZING YOUR ORGANIZATION'S PHILOSOPHY

A thorough analysis of the philosophy of the organizational leadership and various institutional traditions is also needed. As an orientation tool, this analysis may be quite instructive in your first weeks of employment as a facility manager or when new organizational leaders are appointed or employed. Since new administrators are sometimes hired with a mandate to make institutional or program changes, you may need to define and defend your existing management philosophy or adjust quickly to a changing value system.

In exercise 1.2, you will have an opportunity to assess the degree of institutional support for various activities within the facilities you supervise.

Philosophical Changes

If new administrators have been hired to make changes, you must be alert to emerging priorities and the timetable for their implementation. A new institutional philosophy should be reflected in your initial programming initiatives as well as your budgeting and equipment acquisition efforts. An institutional executive who has been hired to reduce costs may well look to the nonacademic components of campus life for budget cuts that will not affect classroom instruction and materials. If this happens, you will need to design policies that focus on preservation of facilities and equipment through programmed maintenance, repairs, careful use, and theft prevention. This effort is more than practical; it is tantamount to survival.

You may find it difficult to implement a philosophy other than your own. However, keep in mind that you are the supervisor who is closest to the facilities, the equipment, and the user groups. You may be able to modify the institutional philosophy if you can demonstrate that the changes you seek are based on widespread customer interests and needs.

Exercise 1.1 Assessing the Impact of Personal Biases on Your Decisions

Assign a numeric value from 1 (high) to 10 (low) to signify how much each of the following factors affects your decision making:

	Impact Rank
	High Low
1. Past athletic experiences as a player	1 2 3 4 5 6 7 8 9 10
2. Past athletic experiences as a coach	1 2 3 4 5 6 7 8 9 10
3. Past instructional experiences as a student	1 2 3 4 5 6 7 8 9 10
4. Past instructional experiences as a teacher	1 2 3 4 5 6 7 8 9 10
5. Past recreational experiences as a participant	1 2 3 4 5 6 7 8 9 10
6. Past recreational experiences as a supervisor	1 2 3 4 5 6 7 8 9 10
7. Past equipment management experiences	1 2 3 4 5 6 7 8 9 10
8. Past facility management experiences	1 2 3 4 5 6 7 8 9 10
9. Other _____	1 2 3 4 5 6 7 8 9 10
10. Other _____	1 2 3 4 5 6 7 8 9 10

Now rank order your biases from 1 (high) to 10 (low) and assess the degree to which they may affect your decisions as a facility and equipment manager.

Impact Rank	Bias Type	Potential to Influence Decisions		
1. _____		High	Medium	Low
2. _____		High	Medium	Low
3. _____		High	Medium	Low
4. _____		High	Medium	Low
5. _____		High	Medium	Low
6. _____		High	Medium	Low
7. _____		High	Medium	Low
8. _____		High	Medium	Low
9. _____		High	Medium	Low
10. _____		High	Medium	Low

Exercise 1.2 Analyzing Institutional Philosophy and Support

To what extent do the institutional philosophy and policies support the following activities?

	Degree of Institutional Support		
1. Required physical education	Low	Medium	High
2. Elective physical education	Low	Medium	High
3. Structured recreation activity	Low	Medium	High
4. Unstructured recreation activity	Low	Medium	High
5. Structured fitness activity	Low	Medium	High
6. Unstructured fitness activity	Low	Medium	High
7. Intramural sports	Low	Medium	High
8. Interscholastic athletics	Low	Medium	High

Follow-Up Questions

What is the likelihood that the institutional philosophy and policies will have an impact on the following activities?

	Degree of Institutional Impact		
1. Personnel selection	Low	Medium	High
2. Activity schedules	Low	Medium	High
3. Budgetary allocations	Low	Medium	High
4. Athletic usage of facilities	Low	Medium	High
5. Recreation usage	Low	Medium	High
6. Private sector usage	Low	Medium	High
7. Facility construction	Low	Medium	High
8. Facility remodeling	Low	Medium	High
9. Equipment acquisition	Low	Medium	High
10. Facility and equipment repair	Low	Medium	High

Finally, when lobbying or conducting public relations campaigns with senior administrators, alumni, voters, or politicians, you need an articulate statement of philosophy to demonstrate future directions for various activity programs and the equipment and physical plant needs they will bring.

When developing or modifying a philosophy for facility and equipment management, you may want to use table 1.1 to assess existing campus attitudes, preferences, and priorities. If more than one group needs to use a particular facility, you will need to establish a joint user philosophy and equitable operating policies. A philosophy that emphasizes student fitness will require policies that integrate this concept within curricula and set budgets and procedures for acquiring a wide range of fitness training equipment.

After you identify priorities, you can define goals, objectives, and policies. Then you can implement them through scheduling, budgeting, purchasing, and policy development.

PERSONAL VERSUS ORGANIZATIONAL PHILOSOPHIES

When you are a candidate for employment or involved in planning a new facility or program, you'll want to keep an eye out for institutional philosophies that could create an adversarial climate or attitudes that might conflict with your initial planning and decision-making efforts. You should assess the need for change in your personal philosophy along with the methods you might use to implement or change an institutional philosophy. Exercise 1.3 will help you compare the key values of your personal philosophy with those of your institutional leadership's philosophy.

Philosophical Differences

The institutional philosophies listed below are examples that could create friction and disagreements with your personal philosophy. Note that as a prospective or new facility manager, you might raise certain questions or challenges (in parentheses).

1. Recreational and intramural sports facilities shall exist to provide wholesome outlets for student energies and activity needs. (What about instruction? Competitive athletics?)

2. Activity centers shall exist to enhance the physical well-being of all students. (Through what medium? Athletics? Recreation? Instruction? Combinations of activity? How will/should these activities be balanced?)

3. The student health division will be directly involved in developing prescriptive activity programs for students. (What about elective physical education? Open campus recreation? Creative use of leisure time?)

4. A healthy mind operates best within a healthy body. (Through what mechanism: Recreation? Personal fitness? Competitive sports? Prescriptive instruction?)

Table 1.1 Priority for Facility Use				
Group priority	Double gym	Multipurpose gym	Swimming pool	Conditioning facility
Athletic priority	yes/no	yes/no	yes/no	yes/no
Instructional priority	yes/no	yes/no	yes/no	yes/no
Recreational priority	yes/no	yes/no	yes/no	yes/no
Private-sector rentals priority	yes/no	yes/no	yes/no	yes/no

Exercise 1.3 Comparing Your Personal Philosophy with the Organizational Philosophy

Rank order the importance of the following from 1 (high) to 6 (low) in the management of sport facilities and equipment.

	Importance to you	Importance to your organization
1. Required instructional activity	_____	_____
2. Elective instructional activity	_____	_____
3. Unstructured recreation	_____	_____
4. Intramural competition	_____	_____
5. Fitness activities	_____	_____
6. Athletic competition and practices	_____	_____

Compare the rankings in each column. Where are there extreme differences? Where are there similarities?

_____

_____

_____

_____

Can these differences be reconciled informally? Do they call for a joint review of program, facility, and equipment needs and program directions? If so, who should participate in this review?

_____

_____

_____

_____

Write a statement of your personal philosophy that is compatible with the institutional philosophy and the priorities you cited above.

_____

_____

_____

_____

5. Athletic facilities will be separate from recreational and instructional facilities and will be constructed, maintained, and supported by athletic contest revenues and by fundraising programs conducted by the athletic department. (Is the facility manager expected to participate in the fund-raising? What expertise is required? What time commitment is expected?)

6. The activity center will be self-sustaining. Revenues from user fees will determine the nature of the program, the type of equipment acquired, maintenance and repair schedules, salaries and benefits paid, and overall profitability. (What about user interests? How will they be assessed? What roles do users play in determining program components and directions? What is the manager's role in making these determinations?)

A Philosophical Clash

You are a new facility director and believe you will serve a greater number of students by creating an intramural sports program that would take place Monday through Thursday between 6 P.M. and 9:30 P.M. You propose this plan in a staff meeting and are immediately chastised by the athletic director, who is upset that your plan will infringe on athletic practice times. What should be the role of your philosophy in this challenge?

PHILOSOPHICAL PRINCIPLES AND FACILITY PLANNING

Once your philosophical position and that of the institutional leadership have meshed and have been shaped by the needs and interests of various users, you are ready to use specific facility planning and development principles as practical extensions of your philosophy.

Theoretical Applications

I suggest several theoretical models as tangible applications of philosophy.

1. User groups (teachers, coaches, recreational users) will be directly involved in the planning specifications for new construction or remodeling.

2. The ages of the primary activity participants will give direction to planning for construction and renovation projects.

3. Current and projected demographic information will be considered in determining both the original size of a facility and potential future expansion needs.

4. All activity spaces will be designed with durability, flexibility, versatility, and convertibility as guiding principles. Facilities will be designed to allow for multiple events to be scheduled simultaneously or for rapid facility conversion when events are scheduled in close sequence. Multiple event considerations include various support facilities such as parking lots, rest rooms, food preparation areas, adequate hallways, stairwells, passages, and exits. All facilities not in use at the time of a sport or recreational event must be secure.

5. All potential activity uses will be considered to make the facility maximally useful to the greatest number of groups.

6. Storage, supervision, and security features must be carefully integrated into new construction or remodeling efforts.

7. Heating, cooling, lighting, internal and external communications, energy conservation, and long-range maintenance will be considered in the selection of architectural features and the planning of operating systems.

8. New construction will incorporate architectural features that allow for efficient renovation, upgrading, and cost-effective future additions to the basic structure.

9. Interagency planning (parks, recreation, instruction, and athletic officials) will be conducted to ensure greatest user access while minimizing duplication of facilities in any geographic area.

10. Special needs will be addressed, including activities for physically and cognitively challenged participants and spectators.

11. Community programs such as theater and musical events, school and neighborhood meetings, day-care programs, elections, and banquets will be included in facility planning efforts.

12. In-depth research will be conducted to gather the most current engineering and planning guidelines from state-of-the-art architectural, educational, and athletic projects.

Each of these applications has potential to alter the schedule and emphasis of the programs offered within the facility that you supervise. They may also affect your budget planning priorities, personnel selection procedures, and facility planning initiatives.

Practical Applications

Because institutional philosophies can vary significantly, exercise 1.4 will give you an opportunity to determine how you would implement various management applications compared with three different institutional settings.

RECOGNIZING YOUR ROLE

The following checklists provide insight concerning the role you may be asked to play given two different priorities and philosophies for various campus facilities (instructional versus balanced instructional/recreational use). Note the change of emphasis in daily operations as the philosophical orientation changes.

Instructional Scheduling Priority

This priority emphasizes quality instruction and recreational activity. Private-sector rentals are possible but athletic access is not considered.

1. The scheduling priority will be accorded to elective and professional physical education classes from 7:30 A.M. to 4:30 P.M. Monday through Friday.

2. Recreational users will be accorded priority use on Saturdays from 7:00 A.M. to 7:00 P.M. They will have priority on weekdays (Monday through Friday) from 6:00 to 7:15 A.M. and from 4:30 to 10:00 P.M.

3. Private-sector rentals may be made available on weekends after 7:00 P.M. and Sundays from 1:00 to 5:00 P.M.

4. Instructional budgeting and purchasing priorities will be assigned as follows.

   • Instructional expendables
   • Instructional capital equipment
   • Recreational expendables
   • Recreational capital equipment

5. Instructional personnel selection will be prioritized as follows.

   • Instructors who can teach individual and team sports equally well
   • Instructors who are specialists in dance, aquatics, recreational/leisure sport activities
   • Instructors who can coach in the intercollegiate/interscholastic program

6. Instructional programming priorities will be as follows.

   • A balanced schedule of lifetime/leisure, conditioning, and team sport courses will be offered each quarter.
   • Recreational offerings will reflect traditional seasonal offering patterns after all instructional priorities have been met.

Balanced-Use Instructional/ Recreational Scheduling Priorities

Note a more balanced access by instruction and recreational activity. Again, athletics are expected to use other facilities.

1. Access priorities

   • The recreational program will have access from 5:00 to 8:20 A.M., noon to 1:30 P.M., and 5:00 to 11:00 P.M. Monday through Friday and from 7:00 A.M. to 5:00 P.M. Saturday and Sunday.

Exercise 1.4 Implementing Management Applications in Different Settings

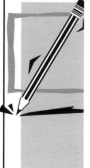

For each key decision in the far left column, there are four columns to the right that reflect four different ways of implementing management applications: one column represents the management priority supported by your institutional philosophy, and the other three columns list the priorities of those decision makers who are motivated by the perspectives of athletics, instructional use, and community access.

Directions: For each of the key decisions, write the activities supported by your management philosophy in the column entitled "Your management priority." Then compare your responses to the priorities of the three other groups.

Key decisions	Your management priority	Athletic priority	Instructional use priority	Community access priority
User group		Athletic teams	Instruction, recreation, intramurals	Scouts, day care, music, drama
Focus of budgetary planning		Uniforms, equipment	Required and elective physical education equipment	Private-sector rental equipment
Program focus		Emphasis on competitiveness	Wider range of offerings in physical education and recreation	Drama, music, civic organizations have increased access
Equipment purchases		Institutional responsibility	Recreation budget	Part of user fee
Personnel decisions		Emphasis on quality coaching	Emphasis on instructors and recreation supervisors	Custodial overtime
Revenue sources		Institutional and gate receipt support	Department budget	Rental fee
Building or remodeling emphasis		Emphasis on athletic and spectator facilities	Emphasis on instructional facilities	Emphasis on multipurpose centers
Source of funding for construction		Institution funded, alumni funded	Bond referendum	Bond referendum

- The instructional program will have access from 8:30 to 11:30 A.M. and from 1:30 to 5:00 P.M. Monday through Friday.

2. Balanced budgeting and purchasing priorities

- Budgets for instructional and recreational supplies and equipment will be shared and apportioned equally.
- Capital construction, remodeling, and equipment acquisition will consider the needs of both the instructional and recreational programs.

3. Instructional personnel priorities

- Comprehensive professional preparation and participation backgrounds will receive strongest consideration in the selection of supervisory and instructional personnel.
- Instructors who are proficient teachers of a wide range of lifetime/leisure, team, and recreational activities will receive highest priority in staffing decisions.
- Specialists whose primary teaching and supervisory proficiency is in the area of team sports will be assigned a lower priority in staffing decisions.

4. Balanced scheduling

- Equal time will be allocated to recreational and instructional program users.

Program Implementation

As the director, you will ultimately be responsible for program implementation, even though most activities will be conducted by subordinate activity supervisors and officials. You can best ensure quality programming by carefully designing supervisor job descriptions, conducting thorough employment interviews, and regularly monitoring and evaluating program supervisors' performance.

Usage Policies and Maintenance Procedures

Efficient facility and equipment usage policies and maintenance procedures are additional tasks for which the director is ultimately held accountable even when these tasks are delegated to staff members. These tasks may be as important as any other supervisory responsibilities because of their impact on user satisfaction and well-being. Clean, attrac-

tive, safe facilities increase customer satisfaction, reduce liability, and improve cost-efficiency. These daily management tasks include maintenance, repair, cleaning, security, safe usage, proper storage, and ongoing inventory of capital and small equipment items.

Assessment

As director, you will institute changes in philosophy and programs based on qualitative and quantitative assessments of user group opinions, interests, and needs. You will need to develop valid and reliable assessment instruments for gathering these opinions.

Budget Planning

Annual budgeting and planning efforts may be the most challenging tasks you will face each year. The need to initiate high-demand programs and acquire modern equipment while responding to local user interests is made more complex by an ongoing requirement to maintain or replace worn equipment and damaged facilities. The need to contain costs while simultaneously managing unforeseen operating system breakdowns demands even greater creative financial and budgetary management.

In order to develop a focused, responsive, and defensible budget, you will need to understand physical plant operating systems and the specific equipment needs of various activity programs. You will also need to know about state-of-the-art methods, technology, and hardware in the fields of management science, sports medicine, and cardiac or physiology research. Moreover, you will have the ongoing responsibility of articulating the current status of these programs, facilities, and equipment and justifying additions or improvements to senior institutional or government leaders. The ability to demonstrate consistency between customer interests and the institutional philosophy can be strategically important.

 **RECOGNIZING THE ROLES OF OTHERS**

The organizational administration must be involved in formulating policy and explaining new policies to user groups (including the underlying or historic reasons for various policies). Because these administrators often have approval authority for budget proposals, they will need to understand the consistency between the department or facility usage philosophy and the size or scope of the budget you are proposing to support the program.

As the manager or supervisor of a sport facility, you must develop, implement, and articulate the institutional philosophy in day-to-day operations with your employees, who will ultimately satisfy (or not satisfy) the facility's users. That philosophy is put into practice through employee interactions with customers on a daily basis, so all employees must receive a thorough orientation to the organizational philosophy and its direct application to all customer services. The following examples amplify this concept.

"I'm a Taxpayer!!"

An irate citizen has asked to schedule a meeting with you. He expects to use the main gymnasium for his youth basketball team's practice and is willing to practice on Saturday and Sunday afternoons when the gym is not heavily used. However, he has been denied access because of the custodial overtime required to open the gymnasium on Saturday and Sunday. He is very upset because he feels that as a taxpayer, he has not only paid the custodial overtime, but he also has paid your salary. He expects you or the custodian to open the gymnasium. What will be your philosophical position?

Administrative Support Minimizes Negligent Liability

High school seniors may believe they should be allowed to practice or compete in a facility without supervision. All personnel who have supervisory responsibility for the facility must be able to explain courteously but firmly that such negligent supervision leaves the institution open to legal liability if anything goes wrong. This policy must be understood and supported at the highest levels of leadership.

Institutional Administrators

The overall institutional responsibility for physical education, recreation, or athletic programs may be assigned to a vice president for campus activities, a dean of student services, a recreation director, an assistant principal, or an athletic director. You must apprise the institutional administrator for your program of your departmental philosophy on facility usage and the ways in which it is implemented at the facility and program levels.

This is an important strategy, because these middle- and upper-level administrators will occasionally receive complaints concerning your program, hear and judge appeals to policy decisions, or process demands for individual considerations. They must be able to articulate a consistent position in support of a particular policy and must understand the reasons for a specific policy or position at issue.

Activity Supervisors

Activity supervisors typically have program-level responsibility and may interact more directly with user groups than any other staff member. Activity supervisors who have specialized areas of responsibility may include

1. the aquatics supervisor,

2. the team sports supervisor,

3. the fitness supervisor,

4. the resistive strength-training supervisor, and

5. the dance supervisor.

These supervisors not only implement the specialized aspects of their program(s) but also are responsible for very important customer interactions. They develop the activity schedule, hire officials and scorekeepers, coordinate custodial and maintenance services, receive complaints, and attempt program-level resolution of customer concerns. Program supervisors also coordinate the schedule of activities under their supervision with other programs that use the same facility and then assess user satisfaction. They also initiate and propose activity budgets and may be authorized to purchase equipment and develop facility management strategies.

Recreation Activity Leaders, Instructors, and Coaches

These individuals have responsibility to implement their respective programs with the athletes, student users, and adult users within the context of the institutional philosophy. They implement institutional policies, assure safe practices, show good judgment, and monitor facilities and equipment. They must receive a thorough orientation to the institutional philosophy and must be able to implement policy in the face of pressure, resistance, and appeal.

Equipment Managers

Beyond their specific equipment issuance and custody functions, equipment managers' interactions with students, faculty, administrators, or private-sector customers can create an environment that enhances or detracts from the satisfaction of these user groups. Courtesy, self-control, and positive communication skills when interpreting philosophy and policy statements to participants can be of immense public relations value. Not all hourly employees or part-time student workers possess these skills. As facility manager, you should teach these abilities and explain the reasons for them with a thorough orientation to the institutional philosophy and policies.

Clerical Workers

Along with preparing concise reports, accurate records, appropriate communications, and accessible files, clerical workers answer customer questions, field and relay complaints, and refer customers to appropriate program or institutional administrators. They occasionally suffer from the "shoot the messenger" syndrome because angry users tend to vent frustrations to the first institutional official they encounter. So these staff members require a thorough orientation as to the need for patience, poise, and tact along with the institutional philosophy and policies. They also need your unflagging support and frequent thanks.

Customers, User Groups, and Participants

You must constantly monitor the satisfaction levels, usage patterns, and preferences of your customers

to ensure that the institution or agency philosophy and program components remain relevant and responsive.

ESTABLISHING GOALS AND OBJECTIVES

When you have established the facility usage philosophy in conjunction with your organizational leadership, you can provide more specific interpretations to program-level workers as the general doctrine moves from an idealized vision to an applications level. To make the transition, goals and objectives are used to specify program dimensions such as activity components, place, time, quantity, and facility or equipment needs. Goal and objective statements can be used to design quantifiable assessments of needs, successes, and customer satisfaction levels; they should be developed and used regularly.

Sample Goal Statements

For discussion purposes, let's assume that the prevailing organizational philosophy specifies that athletic facilities will be separated from instructional/recreational facilities. Given this directional statement, goals can be elaborated in either of these two very different goal statements:

- Athletic ticket revenues and fund-raising initiatives will be the primary funding source for interscholastic sports equipment, supplies, capital construction, maintenance, and remodeling projects.

- Instructional and recreational equipment, supplies, construction, remodeling, and maintenance will be funded with fiscal revenues.

Greater specificity of each goal statement can be achieved with objectives like the following.

- Intercollegiate athletic ticket revenues will be designated to acquire capital and expendable supplies. Athletic construction projects will be accomplished through booster and alumni club fund-raising initiatives.

- Instructional and recreational supplies will be acquired through an annual, prioritized budget process that will be allocated in accordance with state-imposed budget procedures and cost ceilings. Capital construction proposals for instructional facilities will compete with other campus instructional capital priorities.

Summary

To better understand your role as a facility and equipment manager,

1. commit your philosophy to paper to assess its internal consistency and its congruence with the philosophy of organizational leaders or with traditional institutional values;

2. make sure the institutional philosophy and your personal beliefs reflect the needs of consumers and users and give direction to programming, scheduling, budgeting, and personnel decisions; and

3. assess consumer satisfaction regularly so you can respond to consumer needs with continuous evolutions in philosophy, goals, and objectives.

Chapter 2

Assessing Your Facility and Equipment Needs

In this chapter, you will learn

1. criteria for assessing program scope and dimensions,

2. criteria for assessing facility and equipment needs,

3. benchmarks and methods for determining facility and equipment needs, and

4. considerations and methods for balancing needs and resources.

As the manager of highly specialized equipment and facilities, you will need to assess the number and kinds of user groups, the specialized programs and activities conducted, the seasons in which programs are conducted, and the degree to which programs conflict, overlap, or are constrained by the existing physical plant and equipment. This information will help you to implement or modify your philosophy or develop long-range plans for program modification, physical plant construction, renovation, and equipment acquisition.

SIZING UP THE ORGANIZATION

Effective facility management requires that you develop a thorough knowledge of all program dimensions, user needs, and institutional characteristics. You will also need to understand the interaction of these variables over time. Ultimately, participant needs and interests should give direction to your philosophy, goals, and objectives. In turn, your efforts in budgeting, programming, and policy development must ultimately be extensions of your needs-oriented philosophy. Factors to consider include the following.

1. The number and type of user groups (instructional, athletic, recreational, private-sector rentals)

2. The number of sport activities

3. The number of sport activities offered simultaneously

4. The number of seasons in which activities are offered

5. The time required to prepare a facility for a sport activity or season

6. The number of weeks of maintenance and repair activity required or scheduled

7. Long-range construction and capital remodeling planned

8. Major internal system repairs or replacements planned

Identifying the Scope and Size of Program Offerings

In order to develop responsive programs and to acquire appropriate equipment, you must consider the number and type of programs that will be conducted within your physical plant facilities. Find out which instructional, recreation, intramural, competitive sport, and private-sector rental groups will require access to the facilities and specialized equipment inventories.

Form 2.1 (see page 24) asks you to ascertain the number and type of programs sponsored, the seasons in which these activities are conducted, and the frequency with which the activities are offered. To show you how to complete this form, we've filled in the information for the first two facilities.

DETERMINING EQUIPMENT AND FACILITY NEEDS

Each of the considerations in form 2.1 must be examined in light of the specific programs and needs of a particular campus or institution. The following sections look at important subcomponents: facility needs per sport and between sports, the seasons in which activities are offered, time required to prepare facilities, and equipment needs per sport and between sports.

The more popular your facilities are, the more frequently they will need maintenance. Implementing the maintenance and repair program described in chapter 5 will greatly enhance the readiness of your facilities.

Identifying Facility Needs per Sport

User groups vary in age, maturity level, interests, and motivations, and their activities range from highly structured sport competition to unstructured recreation. As a manager or director, you must schedule programs and activities within facilities that are appropriate in size, configuration, and ceiling height and that are equipped with the appropriate hardware and appliances for playing, scoring, and timing various sports. You must also correlate total school enrollment, the size of individual sections, the age and maturity of participants, and the nature of the activities. To offer a comprehensive program of activities, especially during the transition between seasons or between sport practices, you must also consider the ease with which equipment can be set up, stored, moved quickly, and distributed to various facilities.

For safety, you will need to ensure that adequate floor size, field space, and buffer zones are available within and between each facility or playing field and that they are appropriate for the age and competitive level of the participants. Factor in the skills, knowledge, and ratio of supervisors to students as well. When seasons overlap, you will need to schedule activities creatively to avoid conflicts in the activity sites and in such auxiliary spaces as locker rooms, training rooms, and storage spaces.

Comparing Facility Needs Between Sports

You will need to give focused attention to scheduling when several activities are offered simultaneously. Your assignment of spaces and facilities to various user groups must be governed by the number of participants and the types of activities that are offered in adjacent spaces. For example, a class of 23 dance students will need less floor space and ceiling height than 36 volleyball players.

The physical condition of these facilities and the participants' levels of skill may dictate certain choices in assigning activities for practice, competition, or open recreation. Varsity basketball players should be assigned to the spectator gym because of their size, strength, and physical abilities. Conversely, freshmen and junior varsity players may be assigned to a middle-school gymnasium for practice even if they play their games in the spectator facility. During the competitive season, you will need to develop procedures that ensure access to the separate locker spaces by teams that are competing and practicing on the same afternoon or evening. This consideration becomes especially important if a visiting team is assigned to use a locker room that is regularly used by a host school team of the opposite gender.

Shared storage space will also be a concern. You must plan for the security of uniforms, warm-ups, and valuable equipment in conjunction with various activity supervisors. In addition, your scheduling and access plans must comply with the provisions of Title IX of the Education Amendments Act of 1972 and the Americans With Disabilities Act (ADA).

Form 2.2 (see page 25) asks you to correlate these factors to assess needs and assign facilities for each sport.

Seasons in Which Activities Are Offered

The demands placed on maintenance personnel, field caretakers, and equipment managers are magnified when sport seasons overlap or when only minimal periods are available for programmed maintenance.

Preparation and marking of outdoor fields and track facilities, indoor and outdoor painting, maintenance and cleaning projects, and dual use of equipment by various sport teams, physical education classes, or recreation users place inordinate pressure on these support staff personnel. You must also plan for the purchase, acquisition, inventory, and movement of numerous sports equipment items for physical education, recreational, and competitive activities.

Time Required to Prepare Facilities

When competitive sports activities use the same facilities as recreation and instructional programs, the schedules of custodians and other service personnel must be carefully developed to avoid conflict and public relations problems. Here are some time-sensitive facility operations:

1. Preparing bleachers (wall mounted pull-outs and portables)
2. Returning jointly used equipment to proper storage areas
3. Replacing scoreboard lights between competitive events
4. Repairing public address equipment between competitive events

5. Preparing joint-use fields (e.g., soccer and football) with appropriate markings and making the right field equipment ready between competitive events.

Identifying Equipment Needs per Sport

You must regularly assess the equipment needs of the various sports and activities that use facilities for which you are responsible. It is important to subdivide your assessments and assignments into two equipment categories.

1. Capital equipment: permanent equipment or fixed equipment of a permanent or semipermanent nature. For example:

   - Scoreboards
   - Retractable containment nets (tennis, golf)
   - Gymnastics apparatus and floor anchor plates
   - Exercise/wrestling mats
   - Swimming lane lines
   - Volleyball nets, poles, and sleeves
   - Starting blocks
   - Pole-vault and high-jump standards, hurdles
   - Pitching machines
   - Soccer or team handball goals

2. Expendable supplies and materials: materials that have a short life span and require regular replacement. For example:

   - Sport balls
   - Bats, bases
   - Hockey sticks, pucks
   - Scrimmage vests
   - Bows, arrows, target faces
   - Racquets, shuttlecocks
   - Batons, shot put and discus implements
   - Whistles, stopwatches
   - Golf clubs, tees
   - Tennis racquets

Your ability to correlate the specific equipment needs of each sport with appropriate sport facilities, capital equipment, and expendable equipment inventories can expedite the scheduling process and enhance participants' enjoyment. Form 2.3 (see page 26) provides a mechanism for anticipating the equipment needs of various sport activities throughout the school or calendar year.

A sport-specific version of this form is shown in figure 2.1.

Comparing Equipment Needs Between Sports

The contemporary economic climate demands consistent implementation of a universally accepted management philosophy: cost-effectiveness. A practical application of this philosophy involves requiring the sharing of equipment by the various groups that conduct activities in your facilities. Sharing of capital and expendable equipment items can be cost-effective from several standpoints. Cost savings can be achieved by the following.

Cost-Effective Ways to Share Equipment

1. Joint use of instructional and athletic equipment

2. Joint use of men's and women's athletic equipment

3. Joint use of instructional, recreational, and/or intramural equipment

4. Cost sharing for instructional, recreational, and athletic activities

5. Bid or bulk purchasing for instructional, recreational, and athletic activities

---

Some detractors may suggest that sharing equipment will simply accelerate the rate of deterioration or increase the possibilities for loss and theft. But the money you save by not requiring separate inventories and storage spaces will demonstrate your ongoing commitment to cost-effectiveness and your stewardship in the use of public or private school revenues. A critical factor in this concept is holding all supervisors and user groups accountable for security and replacement of equipment that is lost or stolen as a result of negligent management or supervision.

Form 2.4 (see page 27) will help you identify expendable equipment usage patterns among various sports. Form 2.5 (see page 28) will help you assess capital equipment needs.

Sample Equipment Needs Chart for Wrestling

Aug	Sep	Oct	Nov	Dec	Jan
Weight room D	Mats unrolled Q	Inspect uniforms Q	Mats D	Mats D	Mats D
Recondition mats A	Weight room D	Helmets D	Helmets D	Helmets D	Helmets D
Return mats A	Check scoreboard A	Weight room D	Locker room D	Locker room D	Locker room D
			Scale D	Scale D	Scale D

Feb	Mar	Apr	May	Jun	Jul
Mats D	Recondition mats A	Order new equipment A	Weight room D	New equipment arrives A	Weight room D
Helmets D	Recondition helmets A	Repair scoreboard A			
Locker room D	Uniforms to laundry A			Weight room D	
Scale D					

A = annual; Q = quarterly; D = daily

Figure 2.1   Sample equipment needs chart for wrestling.

 # BALANCING NEEDS AND RESOURCES

In balancing available resources with user interests and needs, you will need to use a decision-making rationale that extends the greatest service and access to the largest number of users. When public facilities are built or remodeled, tax revenues, long-range capital construction or remodeling proposals, and annual capital maintenance budgets may be supplemented by donations, bequests, or research grants.

Your role in soliciting these extramural funds must be clarified during the employment process. In some instances, corporate assistance can be encouraged as a tax incentive to business leaders and corporate boards. Fund-raising initiatives can also capture the enthusiasm and zeal of communities or an entire state if you can explain the facilities' benefits to local patrons and potential contributors.

Limiting Factors

During times of economic hardship, referenda aimed at assembling funds for capital construction, remodeling, and equipment acquisition must be carefully considered. The cost/benefit of referendum funds to a broad spectrum of user groups must be documented to show the value of this public investment.

By contrast, private-sector borrowing initiatives will encumber a state or community with interest rates on long-term loans that will eventually require passing these higher costs to taxpayers or to students through increased annual fees and program assessments.

Determining Resources Available

Budgeting is one of the most challenging and creative opportunities you will need to demonstrate your management skills. Some of the variables that will require your ongoing involvement in the budget planning process are listed here.

1. Priority setting that evolves from existing philosophies. What program components require enhancement in order to fully implement the institutional philosophy regarding activity offerings?

2. Use of long- and short-term goals and objectives to focus on priorities. What program goals can be achieved through annual budget expansion? Through capital construction and

capital equipment acquisition? Through long-range borrowing and debt service?

3. Development of equipment acquisition plans based on on-hand inventories. In turn, these inventories and projections must be correlated to enrollment projections and user needs.

4. Reference to documented interests and needs of user groups. Data from participant interest surveys must be gathered and analyzed.

5. Shared funding with other organizational user groups (recreation, intramurals, physical education). Correlated funding plans that reflect joint or separate usage of facilities and equipment must be developed.

6. Supplemental funding by agencies or entities outside the organization. State, federal, and corporate grants can be sought through competitive applications. Supplemental funding groups (booster clubs) can facilitate equipment acquisition and facility construction.

7. Spending or revenue ceilings imposed by government agencies.

Who's Accountable?

The recreation department and the instructional program use the same inventory of basketballs and volleyballs. After three weeks of use by both programs, the physical education teachers indicate that the recreation supervisors have not been monitoring the use of equipment by recreation users. As a result, the basketball inventory has been seriously depleted. What is the role of assessment and supervision in this case?

The National Interscholastic Athletic Administrators Association has published a reference entitled *Managing, Promoting, and Marketing Interscholastic Athletics* that may be of assistance in this area. You can contact the association at the National Federation, 11724 NW Plaza Circle, Kansas City, MO 64195.

Balancing Needs and Resources

You are employed in a state where the state legislature has imposed a revenue ceiling and you are limited to a 2.5 percent budget increase. As you assess your equipment and facility, you find that your budget will be approximately $10,000 short of the funds needed to meet the needs of your participants. What are your program options? What are your funding options?

Facility Needs

In current economic circumstances, proposals to build or renovate facilities will be most successful if you can minimize the impact on taxpayers while demonstrating widespread benefits to large numbers of users.

To minimize fiscal pressures when proposing facility renovation, new construction, or the acquisition of capital equipment items, consider the following funding sources.

1. Long-range capital borrowing and budgeting

2. Annual capital budgets

3. Bequests

4. Gifts

5. Fund-raising initiatives

6. Dedicated ticket revenues

7. Corporate funding

8. Federal or health institute grants

Equipment Needs

You must also develop a plan for regularly acquiring new equipment to replace worn items and reflect emerging user interests. Joint funding of expendable items by the instructional, recreation, intramural, and athletic programs can soften the impact of budget cuts or of cost ceilings and revenue constraints imposed by a municipality or state.

Documentation of long- and short-term acquisition plans, equity initiatives, and support for new programs provide substantive support for annual budget proposals. Consider the following sources of funding for expendable equipment items.

1. Annual supplies and materials budgets
2. Organizational joint funding allocations (instruction, recreation, intramurals, athletics)
3. Booster club support
4. Contest revenues
5. Advertising revenues (media, contests)
6. Gifts

Summary

To assess your facility and equipment needs and limitations, you should

1. define the scope and size of program offerings to identify any deficiencies between user needs and existing facilities and equipment;

2. assess specific equipment and facility needs for each activity conducted within your facility;

3. ascertain whether various activities can share a common inventory of equipment to extend budgets and control expenditures; and

4. assess the funding available from governmental and supplemental sources. Compare revenues to the costs of projected equipment and facility needs.

▎ Form 2.1 — Program Size Assessment of Various User Groups' Specific Facility Needs

Insert the number of sections that will be required in each season the facility in which these sections will be offered, and the expected frequency of use.

Facility	Required health education	Required physical education	Effective physical education	Professional physical education	Private-sector rentals	Conditioning physical education	Dance instruction
Large spectator facility	6/F/D 6/WW/D	NA	NA	2/F/D	NA	NA	NA
Divided spectator facility	4/F/D 4/WW/D	4/F/D 5/WW/D	2/F/D 4/WW/D	2/F/D	3/F/W (P.M.)	NA	NA
Multipurpose gym							
Swimming pool							
Resistive strength facility							
Aerobics facility							
Dance studio							
Rehabilitation facility							

D = daily; W = weekly; Q = quarterly; SA = semiannual; A = annual; NA = not applicable; F = fall; WW = winter; S = spring; SS = summer

■ Form 2.2 — Identifying Facility Needs by Season

Assign facilities for each sport that are appropriate for the activity, conditioning needs, age, and maturity of competitors. Consider ADA and Title IX requirements in making your assignments.

Season/sport	Spectator gym	Gymnastics gym	Multipurpose	Swimming pool	Resistive strength	Locker room 1	Locker room 2	Locker room 3	Training/rehab facility
Fall									
Volleyball									
Badminton									
Cross-country									
Football									
Girls' swim									
Girls' golf									
Girls' tennis									
Winter									
Boys' basketball									
Girls' basketball									
Wrestling									
Boys' gymnastics									
Girls' gymnastics									
Boys' swim									
Spring									
Baseball									
Softball									
Track/field									
Boys' golf									
Boys' tennis									

▌ Form 2.3 — User Group Equipment Needs

Mark the month in which each activity will be scheduled and how often equipment will be needed.

Activity	Aug	Sep	Oct	Nov	Dec	Jan	Feb	Mar	Apr	May	Jun	Jul
Archery												
Badminton												
Baseball												
Basketball												
Crew												
Cross-country												
Dance												
Football												
Golf												
Gymnastics												
Hockey												
Soccer												
Swimming												
Tennis												
Track and field												
Volleyball												
Wrestling												

D = daily; W = weekly; M = monthly; Q = quarterly; SA = semiannual; A = annual

■ Form 2.4 — Joint Use of Expendable Equipment by Sport Teams, Instructional Classes, Intramurals, and Recreational Activities

Place an *X* under the activity setting categories that can share the use of each equipment item listed in the left column.

	Athletics	Classroom	Intramurals	Recreation
Archery bows, arrows				
Badminton birds, racquets				
Baseball bats, bases, balls				
Basketballs				
Crew oars				
Footballs				
Field hockey sticks, balls				
Ice hockey sticks, pucks				
Golf clubs, balls, tees				
Soccer balls				
Swimming/diving apparatus				
Tennis equipment				
Track and field shot/discus/baton				
Volleyballs				

▌Form 2.5 — Joint Use of Capital Equipment Items by Sport Teams, Instructional Classes, Intramurals, and Recreational Activities

Place an *X* under the activity setting categories that can share the use of each capital equipment item listed in the left column.

	Athletics	Classroom	Intramurals	Recreation
Archery targets				
Badminton poles, nets				
Baseball pitching machine				
Basketball scoreboard				
Crew shells				
Dance tape players				
Field hockey goals				
Golf containment net				
Gymnastics apparatus				
Soccer goals				
Swim/dive timer				
Tennis containment nets				
Track and field				
Volleyball nets and poles				
Wrestling timer				

Chapter 3

Developing a Facility and Equipment Management Plan

In this chapter, you will learn

1. the importance of various legal issues to facility managers,

2. why you should develop and maintain records (including financial, inventory, maintenance, and accident records),

3. how to involve staff members and supervisors in planning for risk management and liability prevention, and

4. the importance of assessment and evaluation in facility and equipment maintenance and repairs.

Once your organizational philosophy is in place and you have assessed the organization's needs and directions, you and your staff are ready to develop focused and responsive plans for managing comprehensive activity programs, facilities, and equipment inventories. Several related factors and sources of information should enter into the development of an effective planning model.

ATTENDING TO LEGAL CONSIDERATIONS

The legal mandates of various federal laws, titles, codes, and statutes are important requirements that you must carefully observe when developing the overall planning model for management of a facility or an equipment inventory. They include

- Occupational Safety and Health Administration (OSHA) regulations,
- Department of Industry Labor and Human Relations Codes (DILHR),
- Title IX and equity considerations,
- the Americans With Disabilities Act (ADA), and
- legal fundamentals that relate to risk management and negligence avoidance.

OSHA Regulations

The federal OSHA codes specify structural and environmental conditions for workers and participants and require your staff to engage in proactive facility and equipment safety inspections. Failure to meet these codes can result in assessment of significant fines and penalties by federal inspectors. For specific information related to codes, policies, and standards, you may wish to contact your state office of the U.S. Labor Department, Division of Occupational Safety and Health Administration.

DILHR Codes

The provisions of the DILHR codes protect the rights and safety of workers. Protective clothing, face shields and respirators, air filters and particulate barriers, tool safeguards, and machinery guards are some of the standards described in this legislation. This information can be important to members of your maintenance and repair staff. Contact your state government's safety and building division for a copy of relevant directives and policies.

Title IX and Equity Considerations

Title IX of the Education Amendments Act of 1972 requires equal opportunities for male and female athletes at the collegiate and secondary school levels in all aspects of competitive sports, including

- locker room availability and similarity,
- competitive schedules, dates, times, and transportation,
- practice times and duration,
- equipment and uniforms,
- coaching expertise,
- officiating quality, and
- auxiliary services (rehabilitation/medical services, strength and conditioning programs, academic counseling).

Each requirement has implications for the design, construction, renovation, and management of facilities, as well as the acquisition of equipment, scheduling of activities, and planning of budgets. While the most stringent applications of this law have been at the collegiate level, district federal courts have supported this mandate in numerous high school challenges as well. Your federal or regional Office of Civil Rights can provide information on various issues and standards.

The Americans With Disabilities Act

The ADA requires facilities to offer equal access opportunities for physically and cognitively challenged citizens. The provisions of this federal legislation are still being interpreted by the courts and various institutions. However, it is clear that the intent of this law is to resolve several issues for physically and cognitively challenged citizens. Among them are

1. opportunities to compete in mainstream programs when possible,
2. opportunities to participate in modified programs when mainstream participation is not possible,
3. implementation of adapted methods that ensure adequate transportation, modified competitive equipment, or specialized playing rules, and
4. removal of spectator barriers, and provision of
   - entry gates, turnstiles, and aisles wide enough to allow wheelchair movement and turns,
   - barrier-free viewing areas,
   - shower room and bathroom access (sinks, toilets and toilet stalls, paper dispensers),
   - telephone access,

- door handle access,
- drinking fountain access,
- floor and ramp spaces that are free of wheelchair barriers (grates and water drains),
- appropriate grade or inclines on access ramps,
- appropriate signage to direct patrons with disabilities,
- elevators with accessible controls,
- adequate lighting for participants with visual impairments, and
- adequate ventilation for participants with respiratory impairments.

These can be costly projects and require careful attention to federal, state, and local codes and standards. These considerations will be particularly important during long-range budget planning efforts, especially for major renovation or new construction projects.

Risk Management and Negligence Avoidance

The planning and supervision practices of facility managers must take into account risk management. The basic concept is that everyone assigned or delegated these overall responsibilities has several legal duties or obligations to provide a safe environment for participants. These standards contain several implications for practice; each has evolved from case law findings or legal judgments. These legal duties are

- to plan properly,
- to provide competent supervisors who are able to ascertain when participant facilities, equipment, or activities are unsafe,
- to provide a safe environment,
- to provide safe equipment,
- to provide safe activity,
- to structure activity appropriate for the age and physical maturity of participants,
- to warn participants of potential injury or harm,
- to provide competent emergency care in the event of injury,
- to design an emergency response plan, and

- to train and supervise coaches and activity supervisors.

More specific implications for daily practice and supervision are discussed in chapter 6, Managing Facilities: Supervision.

Local Sources of Information

To develop relevant, responsive management plans, you will need to seek input from a number of locally available information sources. This database can help you achieve compliance with statutes and ordinances. Moreover, seeking information from current and past participants and user groups will help you focus on the programs, facilities, and equipment that provide the greatest satisfaction for taxpayers and constituents.

1. Legal precedents can be obtained through research into state and federal court findings and through regular consultation with your organization's legal counsel.
2. Code and federal law standards can be ascertained through research into OSHA, DILHR, and local facility codes.
3. Users' needs and interests can best be determined through regular surveys of their opinions, needs, and suggestions.
4. Historic information can be acquired through meetings with retired organizational leaders and community residents and through alumni surveys.

Other Sources of Information

Research professional journals, consult with professional experts, research trends in other professional organizations, and meet with staff members and support personnel on a regular basis to acquire information about

1. historic traditions, precedents, and standards,
2. equipment needs,
3. repair and maintenance needs,
4. program needs and interests,
5. security needs, and
6. safety and liability prevention needs.

KEEPING AND USING RECORDS

Records provide important data with which you can document your program successes, your equipment or facility needs, and the interests of your participants. In the following sections, I illustrate some practical applications of record use.

Budgeting

Documentation of need and legal mandates are important criteria that can give direction to your planning and budgeting efforts. This management practice becomes particularly important when you attempt to justify new budgetary proposals or significant increases in total expenditures. A first step is to gather data, conduct surveys, and compile records that you can draw on during planning efforts with your staff and executive leadership.

Important statistical records you can use to demonstrate need or to justify budgetary growth include the following.

1. Total participation statistics
   a. by gender
   b. by age group
   c. by facility (with analysis of square footage needs and usage)
2. Specific activity participation data
   a. instructional activity
   b. recreational activity
   c. competitive sports
   d. correlations of instructional, recreational, and competitive activities by month, day of week, and time of day
3. Specialized participation data
   a. adapted sports
   b. specialized equipment (e.g., resistance strength, aquatics, or gymnastics equipment)
4. Types of adapted equipment required
5. Types of adapted facilities required

6. Revenues generated by various programs that offset expenditures
7. State or federal grant funds available for health research or adapted programs
8. Revenues generated from participant fees
9. Specific provisions of federal or state law that require equipment acquisition or facility modification/construction
10. Per-capita cost analyses (demonstrate financial impact before revenues are collected and net costs after revenues are used to offset costs)
    a. of each activity
    b. by gender
    c. by adapted participant
11. Satisfaction/dissatisfaction survey data from various user groups
12. Cost categories
    a. salaries
    b. equipment and uniforms
    c. capital acquisitions
    d. capital maintenance
    e. annual equipment acquisitions and replacements
    f. annual maintenance and repair
    g. equipment cleaning
    h. transportation

Gathering Previous Records

Figure 3.1 provides a checklist of records that you will find helpful in developing a comprehensive record-keeping system.

Maintaining Records

All of your activity supervisors, coaches, instructors, and equipment managers should be required to maintain records that document the inspection of facilities and equipment on a regular basis. This information is particularly important in developing long-range plans for purchasing, maintaining, replacing, and repairing equipment. These records should include the following information.

1. Size of the facility in which activity is conducted

Records Checklist

1. Accident reports
2. Athletic records
   - Physical exam
   - Parent permission
   - Medical insurance
   - Emergency treatment permission
   - Health insurance
   - Eligibility records
3. Budget history (capital supplies and materials)
4. Inventory of capital equipment (number of units, date purchased, condition)
5. Inventory of sport-specific equipment (number of units, condition)

6. Private-sector user rental record (membership fees, locker rentals, equipment purchases)
7. Swimming pool chemistry check
8. Swimming pool health department check
9. Physical plant facilities checks (date/condition)
   - Lights
   - Ventilation
   - Heat
   - Air conditioning
   - Humidity control
   - Floor
   - Roof
   - Painting

Figure 3.1   Records checklist.

2. Number of storage areas within the space
3. Type and number of equipment items in inventory
   a. by age and condition
   b. by size
   c. whether jointly used for more than one activity (recreation, physical education, athletics)
4. Type and number of capital equipment items within a facility
   a. age
   b. condition
5. Plans for replacement (one-, two-, and three-year plans)
6. Plans for maintenance or repair
   a. noncapital equipment
   b. capital equipment
   c. facilities
   d. facility systems (heating, air movement, lighting, electrical, scoreboard, sound systems, pool systems, and bleachers)
7. Accident records (for planning, remodeling, or equipment acquisition to enhance customer safety)

A Toothy Problem

An athlete comes to your office three weeks after the season ends. He says he was elbowed during a basketball game and as a result has a cracked tooth. The tooth is not readily visible unless inspected by a dentist, and the athlete says he didn't notice the problem until food got into the damaged portion and caused an infection.

You talk to the coach, who says he remembers the athlete receiving an accidental blow to the face during a game but that he heard no more about the injury after it was evaluated by the trainer and treated with ice. A dentist says the tooth needs a root canal procedure, which will cost several hundred dollars. The athlete's family has no dental insurance. The athlete is requesting that you assist him by submitting a claim under the school's athletic insurance policy.

What was the role of the trainer? The basketball coach? What is your role now? What records should you seek to verify the claim?

INVOLVING MEMBERS OF THE ORGANIZATION

Supervisors, coaches, and instructors should meet with the facility manager at least annually to develop individual plans for activity offerings, equipment purchases, facility access, scheduling, and staffing. The total faculty, staff, or department should meet at least quarterly to coordinate the scheduling of facilities and to explore methods for joint funding, staffing, and program planning. Participant satisfaction surveys should be conducted among all users and staff members in order to focus on areas of highest need.

Defining and Sharing Responsibilities

The adage that "a coach is as good as the squad members" is true in the profession of facility and equipment management. As a manager or director, you should select personnel who share your philosophy and who will implement or design procedures and policies that reflect it. Then you should define their duties and responsibilities with detailed job descriptions that will ultimately form a basis for regular evaluation.

Evaluations, in turn, should focus on job expectations. The manager should act as an advocate for the organization but also as a support agent for workers who need assistance in achieving organizational goals. Regular meetings with staff members are important in order to assess program status, movement toward organizational goals, and the assistance or resources that workers need. Customer satisfaction is the primary evaluation criterion.

Form 3.1 (see page 36) provides a planning matrix for involvement of important staff members and facility users.

PLANNING FOR EVALUATION

Facilities and equipment must be evaluated on a regular basis for maintenance tasks such as painting, floor resurfacing, ventilation, electrical, plumbing, locker and pool repairs, and facility sanitizing. The stability, safety, utility, cleanliness, and completeness of all equipment used in daily activity programs will determine the expenditures committed annually to replacement, repair, and maintenance.

Frequent evaluations can help reduce damage and wear that accumulates through long-term inattention. In school settings, much of this work must be accomplished during the summer months, so long-term planning is needed to assign various responsibilities to school or private-sector maintenance workers or to contract with private companies for specialized services. In private-sector activity centers, work can be scheduled throughout the year if facilities and equipment are available to allow short periods of alternative scheduling.

In either case, the institution's annual investment in maintenance and repair activities may depend on the quality and regularity of assessment of the physical condition, safety, cleanliness, and functionality of the facilities and equipment.

Evaluation Timelines

Form 3.2 (see page 37) is a planning matrix that can help your staff coordinate the repair, cleaning, and maintenance plans for your physical plant and service systems with the instructional, competitive, and recreation program calendars. Because some of these renovation projects will require competitive bids and contract letting, early attention to this task is extremely important.

Summertime Blues for a New Coach

A new football coach joined your staff during the summer months. You were on vacation when he reported for work. No one was present to help orient the new staff member to facilities, procedures, and equipment inventories. When the coach opened the equipment room, he was overwhelmed by the odor of mildew and decay. Old equipment has not been inventoried. Equipment with some remaining utility has not been reconditioned or cleaned. New equipment has not been ordered. The season will start in four weeks and there is little time to obtain equipment other than standard items such as footballs and off-the-shelf protective equipment, which will not provide for individual size distributions.

You hired this individual to improve student enthusiasm for and commitment to the football program. What will be this coach's chances of getting off to a good start? Did you and other staff members have any responsibility to make sure the coach received a thorough orientation? What responsibility did you have for equipment inventories or for cleaning, reconditioning, and ordering new equipment?

You will also need to develop calendars and timelines for equipment reconditioning, repair, and replacement with members of your staff. If reconditioning agencies will be hired to do this work, exact specifications of the work to be done, including quality specs, must be clearly stipulated in contract provisions. The calendar dates for equipment pickup and return must be clearly specified to ensure proper transfer of items to the reconditioning company. This timeline must also identify the expected return date so you can make arrangements to receive and store repaired equipment. This latter point is particularly important if equipment will be returned during the summer vacation period. Form 3.3 (see page 38) provides a framework for staff planning for equipment inventory and assessment.

Summary

To develop a facility and equipment management plan,

1. become familiar with legal research and consultation (federal laws, codes, state laws) to make sure planning efforts are guided by relevant mandates, standards, and regulations;

2. develop a record-keeping system that includes participation statistics, participant satisfaction levels, logistics information, and financial data that will stand up to scrutiny;

3. ensure that staff members focus on common standards rooted in an organizational philosophy focused on risk management and participant needs and interests; and

4. involve staff members and users in regular planning and assessment of your programs, facilities, and equipment to help you gain the broadest perspective concerning needs, current and long-range strategies, and innovations in all program areas.

▌Form 3.1 — Planning Matrix

For each planning function listed at the top, place a P after the title of each agent who should be directly involved in planning and a C after those agents who should be consulted.

	Policy development	Facility evaluation	Equipment evaluation	Budget planning	Program planning
Administration (president, chancellor, dean, principal)					
Manager (head coach, facility owner)					
Supervisor (assistant coach, activity supervisor)					
Student (college, high school)					
Faculty					
Adult users (physical education users, parents)					
Employees (equipment managers, custodians, trainers)					

■ Form 3.2 — Facility Evaluation and Maintenance Matrix

Indicate months of evaluation (E), maintenance (M), budget planning (B), and repair (R).

	Aug	Sep	Oct	Nov	Dec	Jan	Feb	Mar	Apr	May	Jun	Jul
Artificial surface track and jumping areas												
Outdoor fields												
Spectator facility												
Multipurpose gym												
Indoor pool												
Outdoor pool												
Resistive strength facility												
Aerobics facility												
Dance facility												
Rehabilitation facility												

▌Form 3.3 — Equipment Inventory and Assessment Matrix

Indicate months of inventory (I), reconditioning (R), and budget planning (B).

	Aug	Sep	Oct	Nov	Dec	Jan	Feb	Mar	Apr	May	Jun	Jul
Archery												
Badminton												
Baseball												
Basketball												
Crew												
Golf												
Gymnastics												
Hockey												
Soccer												
Softball												
Swimming												
Tennis												
Track and field												
Volleyball												
Wrestling												

Part II

Implementing and Evaluating the Facility and Equipment Management Plan

FACILITY AND
EQUIPMENT
MANAGEMENT
PLAN

Chapter 4
Managing Equipment

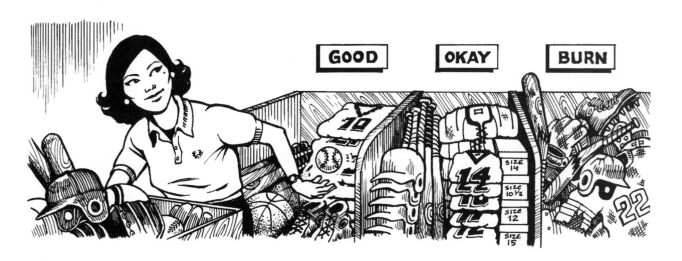

The quality, quantity, and variety of sports equipment that you make available to your participants will help determine the enjoyment they derive from the instructional, recreational, and athletic programs your institution sponsors. In your comprehensive task of managing sport or recreational facilities and equipment, you will have opportunities to demonstrate creativity and innovative leadership as you acquire a wide range of equipment items that directly respond to the interests of your participants. Whether you are directing a high school, college, recreational, or athletic program, the task of managing equipment inventories will ultimately affect your efforts in budget development, program supervision, personnel management, customer relations, and risk reduction.

In this chapter, you will learn

1. how to purchase equipment,
2. how to store equipment,
3. how to distribute equipment,
4. how to repair equipment, and
5. how to evaluate your equipment management plan.

PURCHASING EQUIPMENT

Whether you use a zero-based or incremental budget as a basis for annual budget proposals, at some point in the budget development process you will need to refer to on-hand equipment inventories. You must draw on data regarding the numbers, age, and condition of various consumable and capital equipment items. You must also factor in the normal life span of equipment when considering the cost-effectiveness of maintenance as opposed to replacement. Documented participant demand for various equipment items can help you formulate decisions and proposals. As suggested in earlier chapters, you can gather this information by conducting regular program evaluations and customer satisfaction surveys.

Important Components of the Inventory Process

In any inventory effort, you need to dedicate adequate time and effort to several key components of the larger process. Presenting data that show that your requests for new or additional equipment are based on customer demands will pay great dividends in developing an effective, data-based budget proposal.

Typically, you will ask your program leaders and specialists to commit time to the tasks of counting, categorizing, assessing, labeling, and marking the equipment items used in their activities. Then the total equipment inventory can be compared to projected needs, documented customer demands, and available budget resources. Figure 4.1 shows a sample equipment storage checklist for a high school football program. Note that the uniform items have been organized into home and travel inventories and have been itemized by number and size.

Determining Equipment Needs per Sport

As suggested in the preceding section, you must involve staff specialists in assessing the needs of each program. Their special expertise in the areas of program development and equipment use will be crucial to customer satisfaction and participant safety. This type of involvement gives instructors and supervisors a sense of ownership and empowerment, which makes them more effective.

Moreover, you need staff members' insights concerning equipment deterioration and replacement cycles in order to develop short- and long-term replacement programs. Form 4.1 (see page 52) is a useful tool to determine equipment needs per sport.

Sample Equipment Storage Checklist for Football

Cabinet 1 Home jerseys (49)	Cabinet 2 Travel jerseys (49)
Medium	Medium
Numbers: 1, 2, 4, 5, 7, 10, 13, 15, 16, 18, 22, 24, 27, 28, 29, 33, 35, 37, 38, 39, 45, 46, 47, 48	Numbers: 1, 2, 4, 5, 7, 10, 13, 15, 16, 18, 22, 24, 27, 28, 29, 33, 35, 37, 38, 39, 45, 46, 47, 48
Large	Large
Numbers: 51, 52, 55, 57, 59	Numbers: 51, 52, 55, 57, 59
Extra large	Extra large
Numbers: 66, 67, 68, 69, 74, 75, 76, 77, 79, 83, 84, 85, 86, 88, 89, 90, 92, 93, 94, 95	Numbers: 66, 67, 68, 69, 74, 75, 76, 77, 79, 83, 84, 85, 86, 88, 89, 90, 92, 93, 94, 95
Warm-up jackets (48)	**Game pants (54)**
Sizes: XXL = 24, XL = 12, L = 12	Sizes: 28 = 6, 30 = 12, 32 = 12, 34 = 12, 36 = 6, 38 = 6

Figure 4.1 Sample equipment storage checklist for football.

Require coaches, instructors, and recreation supervisors use this form to communicate with you about their on-hand inventories, their budget requests, and their long-range purchase plans.

Table 4.1 is an assessment instrument to use with a competitive basketball program. It applies the planning principles suggested in the preceding section. The table is intended as a format for discussion and planning, but it does not cover every circumstance. Note that you should consider the equipment purchase date and condition of the inventory in determining the need for reconditioning or replacement.

Coordinated with the inventory process must be your immediate and long-range purchase plans, which are designed to maintain the program, expand it, or change its direction.

Assessing Current Inventory

Along with the obvious collection, counting, and categorizing procedures, the inventory process must also assess the age, condition, and quality of each item.

These are important steps when you are developing budgets or are asked to justify purchases. Citing the life expectancy, the wear stage, and the exact numbers of equipment items in various categories can also help to validate long-range purchasing plans. This information also allows you to make a more accurate judgment concerning the cost-effectiveness of repair versus purchase of new equipment.

Documentation of age and deterioration becomes even more important with certain types of protective equipment. In some cases, manufacturers will not warranty the protective or shock-absorbing capabilities of equipment items past a designated age. Moreover, the number of years that protective equipment has been in service is important for National Committee on Safety of Athletic Equipment (NOCSAE) reconditioning and recertification of your football or hockey helmet protectiveness.

The quality and condition of equipment items are important assessment factors regardless of age. A

Table 4.1   Basketball Equipment Assessment Form

Equipment item	Purchase date	Number and condition		
		Good	Fair	Replace
Basketballs	1993		12	
	1994		8	
	1995		4	
Home jerseys				
Varsity	1990	12	12	15
Junior varsity	1989		12	15
Freshman	1992		12	15
Home trunks				
Varsity	1990	12	15	
Junior varsity	1989		15	
Freshman	1992		15	
Travel jerseys				
Varsity	1991		15	
Junior varsity	1993		15	
Freshman	1992		15	
Practice jerseys	1994		24	
Practice trunks	1994	12	12	

season of intense exposure to rain, mud, and mildew can damage relatively new shoes, clothing, and protective equipment. These factors can disrupt budget, purchase, and reconditioning plans.

Quality should be at the forefront of your considerations. "You get what you pay for" is a time-proven adage that will require you to engage in continuing research to find the highest-quality equipment you can purchase within your budget. Low-grade equipment at bargain prices may cause your staff and your players to suffer from poor workmanship or accelerated deterioration during inclement weather—which can worsen budgetary stress.

Quantity is the most obvious and frequent consideration of the inventory process. New purchases should reflect program needs in terms of participant numbers, equipment sizes, safety, protectiveness, and resistance to deterioration. Several specific applications of this process should be carefully considered, including

- acquiring appropriate sizes for all competitive levels and participant ages, particularly for contact sports,

- acquiring adequate numbers in all size and functional categories to ensure that replacements are available for lost, stolen, worn, and damaged equipment, and

- acquiring enough contest equipment items to account for differences in competitive levels and playing rule requirements, including footballs, basketballs, soccer balls, resistive conditioning equipment, and shot put and discus implements.

Another quantity issue involves using bulk, bid, and individual item purchasing procedures to acquire the many equipment items needed annually for comprehensive activity programs (instruction, recreation, athletics, conditioning, dance). Competitive purchasing shows taxpayers and your institutional administrators that you are cost-efficient.

Bulk purchasing entails purchasing large quantities of a particular item (usually towels or other cloth goods) in order to gain a favorable item price. In bid purchasing, you specify the size, quality, color, and characteristics of a sport equipment item (such as basketballs) and ask vendors to submit competitive bids. Direct purchasing from an equipment manufacturer can also save money by eliminating the costs associated with purchasing through a local

merchandising outlet. Although individual item purchases may be less cost-effective, personal familiarity with local vendors may help you gain good prices, quality control, and customer service.

Purchasing Procedures

Ordering equipment is a relatively simple task, but it does require attention to detail. You must handle it personally or make sure the employees who do are dedicated to accuracy and to meeting the needs of all programs and all customers. At the collegiate athletic department level, ordering is usually assigned to a full-time staff of employees who work with equipment specifications on a daily basis; this lets you delegate the tasks of purchasing and ordering with confidence. Coaches, instructors, conditioning supervisors, or trainers, however, are usually responsible for researching new products.

At the high school level, the task can be more complex because the coach is usually employed as a full-time teacher and divides time among teaching, coaching, and monitoring equipment. It complicates the task if the head coach is required to order equipment for all competitive levels within a program. Combined assignments in athletics/physical education, athletics/recreation, or instruction/recreation also complicate purchasing—particularly if equipment is to be shared by various programs.

Once you determine your immediate and long-range program needs by comparing participation data to on-hand inventories and by assessing participant interests, you can develop and justify budget proposals. Once final budget allocations are approved, you can issue purchase orders or requisitions (taking care not to exceed authorized budget allocations).

Since purchase orders are promises to pay, they must be supported by adequate resources to allow for immediate payment on delivery. Local vendors may sometimes allow for payment over time, but facility managers should not plan on this unless agreements have already been made.

The timing of equipment orders is also critical. Items needed in the fall season should be ordered in February or March; those for winter sports in May or June; and spring orders by August or September. Ideally, new equipment orders should be initiated at the close of a sport season, when equipment inventories, conditions, and needs are clearest. A complication is the fact that new budget funds may not yet be approved or available.

Purchasing Specifications

Precise specification is necessary in the areas of color, size, numbering systems, and fabric content. Several of these factors may be specified by a catalog number. Unfortunately, various color shadings (e.g., cardinal, crimson, and scarlet) or sizes (XXL and XL) may be identified by sequential numbers that are separated by only one or two digits or letters in the vendor's catalog. For this reason, the orderer must pay close attention to details, especially when ordering a close-out item for which substitutions would cost extra.

When ordering in bulk or letting competitive bids, it is imperative to specify all identifying features or qualities desired. In some cases, you might indicate "no substitutes authorized" for a particular product. When vendors offer substitutes for a particular product, obtain samples for trial use by your staff before buying them.

Insights about product quality can be obtained from user groups, other supervisors, other coaches, equipment managers, and the Athletic Equipment Managers Association (AEMA). Factors to consider include safety records, NOCSAE approval, durability records, the manufacturer's or vendor's customer service records, and timeliness of the delivery system.

You can often save money by ordering early, purchasing close-outs, taking advantage of inventory reductions, and experimenting with new products. In these cases, you will need to be especially cautious about quality, product reliability, and vendor warranties.

Figure 4.2 shows a sample purchase requisition. It includes the sales outlet, specifications, and costs of the ordered items, as well as the total cost, budget to be encumbered, delivery address, and receiving agent.

Equipment Delivery and Receiving

Delivery, receiving, and custody are all important activities that affect equipment security and customer satisfaction. Find out ahead of time whether you or the manufacturer will pay the delivery costs. They can add 2 to 5 percent to the total cost of an order and may present an unpleasant surprise when year-end accounting and auditing procedures are conducted. Find out also the delivery time frame and the contracted trucking firms or rail agents so that custodial personnel or other staff members can be alerted to the approximate arrival date.

The size, weight, and number of items to be delivered may be of concern as well. If a multistation resistive strength-training machine is arriving, enough people, carts, and lifting machines will be needed to offload it safely and expeditiously and move it to the appropriate facility. Tools for opening cartons, inscribing or marking new equipment, and assembling components will also be needed.

Sample Purchase Requisition Form

Vendor: Midwest Athletic
Vendor Address: 2444 Union Ave., Toledo, OH
Salesperson: Bill Thomas
School account number: 10-145-411-162-299
Deliver to: Memorial High School
2301 S. Gammon Rd.
Massilon, OH
Attn: Coach Joe Jones
Items:

24 Rawlings XRT men's basketballs
Ea. $44.95 = $1,078.00

24 Southern jerseys, style 34
Color: Royal blue
Trim pattern: 16
Ea. $38.50 = $924.00

Total: $2,002.00 (shipping included)

Figure 4.2 Sample purchase requisition form.

The Color of Carelessness

You ordered your new basketball uniforms at the end of the last season. The purchase requisition was issued by your purchasing department. The funding codes and the ordering timeline were correct. The uniforms were delivered in June, just before school closed for the summer. You left them in the shipping cartons so there would be no chance of mildew or other damage. Two weeks before the season, you opened the cartons—only to discover that the jerseys are the wrong color. When could you have resolved this problem? Where should you look to find the cause of the problem and to prevent it from recurring?

STORING EQUIPMENT

Beginning with the delivery of equipment, you should designate several people to assist with handling and storage. If equipment is delivered when coaches are not present to receive it, secure storage must be found. One custodial agent should be identified as the primary receiving and security agent. This individual will need keys to secure storage areas and will need to notify instructors and coaches that the order has arrived.

In a college athletic department, a full-time staff of equipment managers typically handles these tasks. Newly delivered equipment should be inspected as soon after arrival as possible to verify that the right colors, numbers, styles, and other specs were delivered.

Equipment is usually stored by category (uniforms, bats, balls, protective equipment, etc.) or by size or competitive level. Regardless of category, equipment should be stored in a dry, pest-free area that is easily accessible to supervisors and participants.

Determining Storage Needs

The need for storage space must be taken seriously because of its potential impact on the condition and accessibility of equipment inventories. You must consider the following factors.

1. The total number of equipment items
2. The size of individual equipment items
3. The need for immediate accessibility
4. The need for rapid conversion from one activity to another
5. The number of athletes who will be processed at the start or end of a season, each practice night, and each contest night
6. The number of items to be issued to each player
7. The need for uniform hanging space
8. The need for overhead bulk equipment storage racks
9. The need for secure storage of items with high theft potential (jerseys, warm-up jackets)

10. Capital equipment items such as wrestling mats, volleyball standards, gymnastics equipment, track and field implements, hurdles and landing pads, soccer goals, football sleds and training apparatus, and motorized carts

Determining Space Available

A number of factors must be considered when you and your staff identify certain spaces as potential storage facilities. Overriding considerations include the safety of participants and equipment managers, the ease of equipment access and distribution, the need for secure storage, and the general impact of the facilities on the condition of the equipment inventory.

Consider the following physical plant factors.

1. Proximity of the facility to activity sites, locker rooms, and coaches' offices can enhance issuance and collection procedures and problem solving.
2. Conversion of unused industrial education or art labs during periods of declining student enrollment can provide additional storage sites.
3. Utility tunnels may also expand storage space; however, they must satisfy OSHA regulations and DILHR standards.
4. Storage garages and outdoor metal sheds can add storage—although weather, humidity, pest control, potential flooding, frost, and sunlight exposure may be problems.

Securing Storage Areas

The value of athletic equipment and tight budgets combine to mandate a security plan for each sport facility. Instructional and activity supervisors, custodians, and equipment managers should be involved in the development of plans and procedures. The following security measures are suggested.

1. Change locks or padlocks in order to control access.
2. Use solid steel padlocks with protected shackles to deter theft.
3. Select areas that are free of frost and ground leakage and removed from swimming pool

surge tanks. If you must use damp areas, install shelving and elevated storage racks.

4. Conserve space by using elevated helmet racks and storage trees.

5. Use cabinet storage for high-demand items such as game jerseys, warm-up jackets, shoes, and contest equipment.

6. Impress upon managers the level of trust that has been accorded them.

7. Don't block the aisles or stairways.

8. Meet code specifications for lighting and ventilation.

9. Install systemwide or room humidity controls.

10. Install smoke detectors and check their power sources regularly.

Methods for Identifying Equipment

Equipment should be marked as soon as possible with bar coding, metal etching, or water-resistant marking. Correlating equipment assets to the year of purchase (e.g., 1-95, 2-95, 3-95; 1-96, 2-96) will help you develop adequate inventories and long-range replacement plans. This is important because certain protective items, such as football helmets, must be reconditioned or replaced within specified time frames and present significant liability issues for coaches and managers who do not comply.

Storing Capital Equipment

Because capital equipment is so expensive, special precautions are needed to protect it against theft, damage, or vandalism. Exercise, wrestling, and floor mats are particularly vulnerable to damage from physical education classes and spectator groups if left in a thoroughfare area. To prevent damage, you may wish to install wall-mounted mat rollers that allow you to store mats above the floor while maintaining cleanliness and minimizing damage.

To change activities rapidly in a multipurpose facility, you need the right size mat carts and apparatus transporters. Large storage closets with large access doors are needed to ensure that equipment such as shock-absorbing landing mats, horses, beams, bars, runways, and ring-support units can be moved quickly and safely. Since architects may

not be familiar with these special needs, teachers and coaches of these specialized activities should be involved in the design or remodeling plans for such facilities.

DISTRIBUTING EQUIPMENT

Distribution of equipment in a school or recreational facility involves several important procedures related to accountability and return of equipment. Distribution of protective equipment for contact sports requires special fitting and wearing procedures.

Accountability

To maintain accountability, identify the equipment user and complete a custody form. In private-sector or recreational settings, user identification cards may be retained by the issuing agent until the equipment item is returned. In school settings, a custody card is completed by the issuing agent and signed by the athlete to validate receipt of specific items.

A custody card should be filled out for each athlete (see figure 4.3). The athlete should sign the card to acknowledge its accuracy and receipt of the equipment.

You might keep a master equipment roster that correlates the player's name and locker number to each equipment item (see figure 4.4). Keeping such a roster in the team room can minimize theft and loss and expedite returning lost equipment to its owner quickly.

Equipment Fitting

Helmets, shoulder pads, thigh guards, and shin guards should be fitted by an experienced person who instructs athletes in the proper wearing of the equipment. This monitoring process is particularly important for younger players and could be a source of negligent liability if not performed carefully.

Computerizing Your Distribution Procedures

Computerized equipment inventory and distribution procedures are very effective. If bar codes are used

Sample Equipment Custody Card

Name: John Smith   Year in school: 1   2   3   4
Home phone: 255-4888   Address: 71 E. Jackson Ave.

Equipment item	Number	Checked out	Checked in
Shoulder pad	27	8/5/96	11/5/96
Hip pad	23	8/5/96	11/5/96
Helmet	44	8/5/96	11/5/96

Athlete signature   Date

Figure 4.3 Sample equipment custody card.

Sample Master Equipment Roster

Name	Locker	Helmet	Shoulder pad	Hip pad	Jersey	Pants
Tom Anderson	12	44	24	35	23	38
John Baker	14	59	34	45	45	49
Leonard Washington	33	61	59	64	72	33
Crawford Henderson	41	33	89	53	84	74

Figure 4.4 Sample master equipment roster.

to distribute equipment to players, the bar-code inventory symbol can be correlated to locker number or player name. Lost-and-found items can be scanned and returned to the proper athlete.

Electronic inventory can also be useful for monitoring equipment type, style, size, purchase date, vendor, reconditioning history, and usage pattern. You can draw on these in developing budgets, purchase plans, and reconditioning programs. Here are three inventory software packages to check out:

Sports Stats Inc.
320 Brookes Dr.
Hazelwood, MO 63042

Recreation Facility Software
4633 E. Broadway
Tucson, AZ 85711

A. D. Software
215 Islip Ave.
Islip, NY 11751

Record-Keeping

Certain data must be maintained in an equipment record-keeping system to assist future purchasing, maintenance, and budgeting procedures. You need to know the total number of equipment items on hand, the date of purchase, size and color distributions, and the number of items assigned to each competitive level or to each recreational or instructional program. Brand names, vendor names, and purchase prices will be important if you want to buy new uniforms or equipment, as will information about whether you used competitive bidding or bulk purchasing. NOCSAE certification dates must be recorded accurately.

At the high school level, responsibility for record-keeping may fall to a designated equipment manager or a head coach. Each of the following equipment operations requires record-keeping.

1. Fitting players

2. Issuing equipment

3. Keeping custody records

4. Collecting equipment

5. Inventorying equipment (ages, colors, sizes, types)

6. Making minor repairs

7. Contracting maintenance with a reconditioning company

8. Handling maintenance

9. Purchasing new equipment

10. Supervising student managers

The individual responsible for record-keeping must be consulted during all purchasing, maintenance, and reconditioning efforts. Record-keeping enhances your budget and management effectiveness because it helps you combine informed equipment acquisition with parallel maintenance planning to improve the inventory. This lets you use resources most effectively to combine new and older equipment while maintaining utility, protectiveness, and appearance over long periods.

REPAIRING EQUIPMENT

As manager of a recreation or school activity facility, you will need to consider a range of regular equipment maintenance and repair activities, including cleaning, sewing, repairing, repainting, resurfacing, rewiring, replacing components, and inspecting systems. Regular inspection and programmed maintenance of expendable and capital equipment are needed in order to operate effectively within tight budgets.

Repair Procedures for Each Sport

Repair procedures vary with the type of equipment used and the stress it receives during practice and competition. Determine cost-effectiveness by comparing the life expectancy of a repaired item to that of a new purchase with warranty. The following options should be analyzed for cost.

- Sewing
- Steam cleaning
- Washing

- Pad replacement
- Strap replacement
- Hardware replacement (buckles, cables, floor plates)
- Cable replacements
- Electronic component replacements
- Mat surface reconditioning
- Landing surface reconditioning
- Protective padding replacement

Among other seasonal matters that your staff must check are the following.

Season Equipment Checks

Preseason/in season

1. Proper fitting

2. Proper wearing and use of equipment

3. Enough equipment items to achieve proper instructional, conditioning, and training goals

4. Deterioration, breakage, and theft of equipment

Season end

1. Collection of all items

2. Inventory of items by type, size, color, and model

3. Equipment cleaning and repairs

4. Decisions on equipment discarding

5. Budget proposals reflecting inventories and participant needs

6. Purchasing, receiving, and storage of new equipment

Relying on annual budgets to replace damaged equipment rather than on repair and maintenance is an inefficient procedure that can be challenged by taxpayers and school administrators. For that reason, the preceding list of procedures must be carefully implemented.

However, this may be a challenging task if your staff consists largely of nonfaculty coaches or supervisors who are not present during the off season.

You may wish to develop a written performance expectation for nonfaculty coaches that specifies these responsibilities as a condition of employment. You may also want to stipulate that seasonal coaching compensation will be paid after all equipment responsibilities have been met satisfactorily.

Cleaning Equipment

Your staff will need to inspect garments for washing instructions. Expensive uniforms can be damaged or faded by the wrong water temperatures or cleaning products. Some uniform items may require dry cleaning and sealed storage. All surfaces that athletes touch during practice, competition, or medical treatment should be cleaned frequently. These include protective padding, helmets, gymnastics and wrestling mats, weight-lifting benches, and trainer rehabilitation equipment. Bloody uniforms and towels must be washed separately or disposed of.

Contest and practice equipment must also be washed on a regular basis (usually weekly). You will need to send capital items (protective helmets, padding, wrestling/gymnastics mats, and other gymnastics equipment) to certified reconditioning agencies for cleaning and repairs, which may require six to twelve weeks.

Figure 4.5 shows a sample timeline for management of various maintenance, repair, and cleaning responsibilities.

Sample Equipment Repair Timeline for Wrestling

<u>Daily</u>

Clean mat with approved antiseptic

Launder bloody towels, uniforms, pads (biohazard containers)

Dispose of gauze, bandages, tape (biohazard containers)

Clean ear protectors with antiseptic

<u>Weekly</u>

Wash singlets

Wash socks

Wash knee pads (unless blood-stained)

<u>Annually</u>

Repair mats

Sew singlets

Wash singlets

Sew warm-up jackets

Dry clean warm-ups

Repair/clean head/ear guards

Repair/clean shoes

Figure 4.5   Sample equipment repair timeline for wrestling.

Financial Austerity

Your administrative supervisor informs you that the board of education has decided to impose a 5 percent budget reduction on the physical education, recreation, and athletic budgets in order to reduce the total impact on local taxpayers. You are expecting record participation in your elective physical education classes, and the recreation and athletic programs have demonstrated stable but extremely large participation levels. You need a plan that will use various maintenance and purchasing techniques to meet the needs of your coaches, supervisors, and participants while staying within the mandates of the budget cut.

EVALUATING YOUR EQUIPMENT MANAGEMENT PLAN

As with all other aspects of facility and equipment management, you will need to assess the effectiveness of your overall plan for purchasing, storing, distributing, and repairing equipment. Components of your plan to be assessed include the following.

1. Purchasing: Do equipment acquisition procedures provide

    a. enough high-quality equipment for instruction and practice?

b. enough high-quality equipment for recreation programs?

c. materials that respond to new and emerging needs?

2. Management: Do management procedures ensure

a. adequate storage and security of equipment?

b. adequate cleaning and maintenance procedures?

c. accurate inventory procedures?

d. efficient use, transfer, and sharing of equipment?

e. effective inventory that is correlated to maintenance and acquisition procedures?

3. Assessment: Are evaluation procedures used to measure

a. customer interests?

b. security procedures?

c. budget and acquisition procedures?

d. inventory procedures?

e. equipment issuance, fitting, and monitoring?

4. Are assessment data used to make equipment selection, purchasing, and replacement decisions?

In the final analysis, you will need to determine whether your plan is consistent with your philosophy and with your immediate and long-range program goals. Regular assessment and comparisons will help you achieve those goals.

Summary

To develop a successful equipment management plan,

1. maintain accurate inventories as a basis for developing justifiable budgets and focused purchasing plans (equipment age and condition are key assessment factors);

2. use purchasing methods designed to derive favorable pricing considerations, including competitive bidding and bulk purchasing;

3. maintain the security and custody of items from the time they are delivered to participants until they are returned for maintenance and cleaning;

4. use good record-keeping procedures to maintain accurate records of use while assigning user accountability;

5. develop efficient receiving, tracking, and security methods; and

6. use accurate assessment of equipment items and systems as a basis for programmed maintenance and repair. Extending the life expectancy of high-demand, heavily used equipment extends annual budgets, elevates public confidence, and enhances customer satisfaction.

▌Form 4.1 — Determining Equipment Needs Per Sport

Assess the number of equipment items in your current inventory, including purchase date and general condition. Compare these figures to your projected program needs.

Sport
Varsity, JV, Freshman
(Circle)

Equipment item	On-hand number	Program needs	Color	Purchase date	Condition Excellent	Fair	Replace
1.							
2.							
3.							
4.							
5.							
6.							
7.							
8.							
9.							
10.							
11.							
12.							
13.							
14.							
15.							
16.							
17.							
18.							
19.							
20.							

Chapter 5

Managing Facilities: Maintenance

As a facility and equipment manager, you are entrusted with maintenance of some of the most popular and costly physical assets within your school district, campus, or physical plant. For this reason, regular inspection and repair procedures must be important considerations in your daily and long-range planning efforts. This management task can also have a major impact on budgeting, customer satisfaction, and liability prevention.

In this chapter, you will learn

1. the importance of short- and long-range maintenance programs,

2. the need to designate long-range calendar dates for maintenance and repair,

3. the importance of assigning responsibilities for preparation of facilities for practice and competition,

4. reasons to conduct regular safety and hazard checks, and

5. how to interact with facility managers of activity sites not under your school district's control.

DETERMINING FACILITY MAINTENANCE RESPONSIBILITIES

Because of the intense demand for indoor and outdoor activity sites, maintenance is an important concern for you. You are responsible for providing or proposing budgetary support for maintenance projects on a regular basis. Some facilities are used by your school but scheduled and maintained by another agency (for example, the city parks department). In such cases, you must arrange for maintenance by these agencies or develop joint funding arrangements.

Facilities Owned or Managed by Other Agencies

Among the specialized facilities that may be owned and operated by other public or private-sector agencies are aquatic facilities, ice rinks, team sport stadiums, and baseball/softball diamonds. You will usually have an annual rental or lease agreement for use of such a facility that specifies the rental or lease rates and any special fees for setup/takedown, cleaning, and maintenance.

You may be required to coordinate access to these facilities in conjunction with the coaches of teams that will use them. Adequate lead time must be incorporated into the planning model to ensure access to these high-demand facilities. Hockey, swimming, and gymnastics facilities are often sought by numerous youth sports groups, all of which make a strong case for access during prime-time practice and competition hours. The amount of time allocated to a renter or lessee is often calculated as a percentage of the total rental time each organization commits to practice and competition within the specialized facility. In this model, the most desirable ice time is allocated to these organizations that commit to the most total rental time.

You will need to dedicate sufficient time to negotiating and requesting capital maintenance, construction, renovation, and completion of building projects before a competitive season begins. This process may require negotiation between the chief executives or governing boards of two government agencies (for example, a school system and a university, or a school system and a parks department), which further underscores the need for adequate planning time.

In some cases, this agreement can be accounted for through annual rental increases. In others, an actual contract for sharing of maintenance costs must be developed. Table 5.1 shows various school and community user groups' degree of responsibility for facility maintenance. Note that the degree of maintenance responsibility is a function of facility ownership and/or primary usage. Note also that agencies that own and manage facilities that your teams use may require you to negotiate a shared maintenance responsibility.

Between a Rock and a Dasher Board

Your hockey coach says he needs new dasher boards at the base of the rink walls in the facility that you rent for your high school contests. You contact the rink manager in September preceding the season, which will begin in November. The manager says she will be unable to do the maintenance this year because the funding allocation for this project was cut from her budget. You ask whether you can transfer funds between agencies to cover the needed repairs. She tells you that the transfer procedure will be acceptable but her maintenance staff will need to do the work. Unfortunately, they will be occupied on a major renovation project until mid-November. You have two choices: You can play hockey in a dangerous facility until repairs are made or you can try to find alternative facilities in which to compete.

DETERMINING TIMELINES

For each of the various facilities that you oversee, certain maintenance tasks must be performed on a regular, short-term basis and others semiannually or annually. It is important that you anticipate these projects because you will need to cancel activities temporarily in those facilities scheduled for service. In school settings, summer months are traditional times to schedule maintenance activities. However, if summer school classes have been scheduled in these facilities, the window of opportunity for maintenance may be significantly reduced.

If several schools or facilities require the same type of major maintenance (e.g., roof repairs) the pressure on various private contractors may mean they can't meet your needs unless you have developed long-range schedules. Table 5.2 illustrates the variability of schedules for various maintenance projects. Note the possibilities for heavy demands on contractors or your own custodial staff for annual or semiannual repairs or maintenance. Note also the possibilities for interference with seasonal sport transitions in those facilities that require quarterly maintenance. For example, both practice and competition may be disrupted if scoreboard, gym lighting, or public address maintenance requires protracted efforts between a fall volleyball season and a winter basketball season.

Staff Responsibilities

As facility manager, you must identify staff members to whom you will assign responsibilities for routine maintenance tasks and for monitoring the conditions of various systems or facilities. Obviously, expertise will play a major role in selecting these staff members. You will need to orient them thoroughly to the narrow windows of opportunity available for maintenance on game nights, between seasons, and during the summer months.

These individuals will have additional responsibility for initiating routine repair requests or for developing budget proposals to support building system replacements or major maintenance projects. Table 5.3 shows the assignment of tasks to various staff members or specialists.

Note that instructors and supervisors must be assigned responsibility for identifying specific maintenance needs. By referring these maintenance tasks to your building repair specialists, you may be able to resolve minor problems and schedule major repairs well in advance to avoid overloads and con-

flicts during the seasonal transitions and summer months.

Seasonal Timelines

You need to be aware of the seasonal timelines for routine and long-range maintenance programs so that you can develop budget proposals to support needed maintenance projects and consult with both building and private contract maintenance specialists about them. Figure 5.1 illustrates a four-season plan for maintaining a wide range of sites, facilities, and equipment. Note that maintenance is generally planned for completion during the off season.

This schedule requires you and your staff to engage in a long-range planning effort that begins with identification of various maintenance needs at the end of each season or unit. The model provides adequate time for planning and budgeting and increases the possibility that private contractors can meet your timelines.

Bidding Timelines

You must solicit specialized bids for maintenance and repair projects for those facilities that require work that is beyond the training and capabilities of your building custodial or maintenance staff. For recurrent maintenance projects, you need enough time to research maintenance agencies, write bid specifications, and receive bids from private repair agencies.

You should begin this process at least three months before a facility or system will be needed. By the time you receive and compare bids and choose one agency, the time left for scheduling and completing work will be only three to six weeks. If this work must be coordinated with other schedules (e.g., summer school; use of the gym to store furniture while classroom floors are resurfaced), the schedule will be even tighter. Moreover, if the services of certain contractors (roofing, heating/cooling firms) are in high demand during a particular season, you need to make early arrangements if you hope to obtain their services at all.

Figure 5.2 illustrates a bid solicitation that requests competitive maintenance proposals from private-sector roofing contractors.

Table 5.1 Agency/Department Facility Maintenance Responsibilities

	Instructional gym	Multipurpose gym	Strength-conditioning facility	Aerobics facility	Dance studio	Outdoor fields	Tennis courts	Pool
Recreation dept.	High	High	High	Possible	Low	Possible	Possible	Possible
Athletic dept.	Low	Possible	Low	Low	Low	Possible	Possible	Possible
Physical education dept.	High	High	High	High	High	High	High	High
Parks dept.	Low	Possible	Low	Low	Possible	Low	High	High

Table 5.2 Maintenance Schedules of Various Facilities

Maintenance project	Competitive gym	Swimming pool	Multipurpose gym	Resistive strength	Aerobics facility	Dance facility	Outdoor fields	Outdoor diamonds
Roofing	1	1	1	1	1	1	1	1
Painting	2	2	2	2	2	2	NA	NA
Floor resurfacing	2	NA	2	2	2	2	NA	NA
Air movement equipment and filters	3	3	3	3	3	3	NA	NA
Heating/cooling	3	3	3	3	3	3	NA	NA
Humidifier	3	3	3	3	3	3	NA	NA
Electrical	3/4	3/4	3/4	3/4	3/4	3/4	3/4	3/4
Scoreboard	3/4	3/4	3/4	NA	NA	NA	3/4	3/4
Public address	3/4	3/4	3/4	3	3	3	3/4	3/4
Competitive lights	3/4	3/4	3/4	3/4	3/4	3/4	3/4	3/4

1 = 5-10 years, 2 = 1-3 years, 3 = Annual, 4 = Quarterly/seasonal, NA = Not applicable.

Table 5.3   Staff Member Assignments Related to Facility Maintenance

Staff member	Cleaning	Painting	Resurfacing	Air movement	Pool system	Heating/cooling system	Electrical system	Scoreboard
Instructor (identify need)	D	D	NA	D	D	D	D	D
Activity supervisor (identify need)	D	D	D	D	D	D	D	D
Custodian	D	D/SA	P/A	NA	P/SA	NA	P/Q	P/W/Q
Building maintenance staff	NA	NA	NA	P/SA	P/A	Q	Q	P
Contract maintenance	NA	P/A	P/A	P/A	P/A	P/A	P/A	P/A

P = Possible, D = Daily, W = Weekly, Q = Quarterly, SA = Semiannual, A = Annual, NA =Not applicable.

Maintenance Timelines

Summer	Fall	Winter	Spring
Roofing	Reseeding and fertilizing fields (late fall)	Painting	Fertilizing fields
Painting		Soccer and football goals	Football and basketball scoreboards prep
Floor resurfacing and hardware	Tennis courts resurfaced	Bids for stadium lights	Public address repairs
Electrical systems	Track and jump surface repairs	Humidifier and cooling system prep	Heating system repairs
Pool system repairs	Heating system repairs	Bids for cooling system repairs	Bids for summer and fall repairs
Stadium light repairs	Diamond maintenance		
Basketball scoreboard prep	Repaint/repair fences and baseball bleachers		
Public address repairs			
Driveway and parking lot repairs			
Watering and seeding fields			

Figure 5.1 Maintenance timelines.

Sample Request for Roofing Maintenance Contract Proposals

The Jefferson School District is seeking competitive bid proposals for the following roof maintenance procedures at the Jefferson High School Athletic Fieldhouse, 1800 Johnson St., Jefferson, MI.

a. Remove 18,000 square feet of asphalt composition roofing.
b. Install 18,000 square feet of waterproof underlayment.
c. Install 18,000 square feet of rubber-sheeting exterior roofing surface.
d. Seal exterior surfaces, sheeting seams, roof-edge surfaces, exterior chimneys, vents, and electrical and electronic fixtures.

All procedures must be accomplished between June 1 and August 1, 1996. Sealed bids will be opened at 2:00 P.M., Friday, May 3, 1996, in Room 105, Doyle Administration Bldg., Madison, WI 54301.

Figure 5.2 Sample request for roofing maintenance contract proposals.

PREPARING FACILITIES FOR INSTRUCTION, PRACTICE, AND COMPETITION

Advance preparation of facilities and equipment will ensure maximum efficiency and time utilization during sports practice sessions or instruction. This same concept applies to preparation of facilities for competition—with the additional considerations of customer safety and satisfaction.

Form 5.1 (see page 62) is a sample facility inspection list that can be used as a planning tool or focus for staff discussion and seasonal inspections.

Whose Fault?

In the high school multipurpose spectator facility, a floor plate support for a gymnastics parallel bar has worked loose and projects slightly above the level of the gym floor (which is also used as the basketball team's competitive surface). During practice, the basketball coach notices the projecting plate and sends a written note to the head custodian requesting repair. Three days pass without repair. On the fourth day, a basketball player dives for a loose ball, slides on the floor, and strikes the corner of the plate. The player sustains a serious laceration, which requires loss of playing time. The player is a Division I scholarship candidate and will lose exposure to several college coaches who have been watching her play. When asked about the maintenance request, the custodian says he did not receive it. Is there negligence in this case? If so, who is the negligent party? What procedure would you suggest to address this issue?

Maintenance Requests

A procedure for requesting maintenance and repairs that uses a multiple-copy form should be developed for your staff members. They will send one copy of the request to the proper repair technician or main-

tenance supervisor, a second copy to your administrative supervisor, and a third to you for your files. This will document the need for budgetary support for major repairs and provide a chronological record of the requests for service you have initiated.

Form 5.2 (see page 63) illustrates a format for a printed maintenance or repair request.

EVALUATING YOUR FACILITY MAINTENANCE PLAN

As you conduct your maintenance program, you will need to determine its success. You and your staff should regularly assess the items on form 5.3 (see page 64).

SITE-SPECIFIC CHECKLISTS

The facility checklists on pages 65-68 have been prepared for 21 instructional or competitive activities. Forms 5.4 through 5.24 are maintenance checklists intended to improve facilities' readiness for practice and competition, including meeting important provisions of the Americans With Disabilities Act. For each checklist, "ADA access" indicates that the facility has been physically prepared, constructed, or renovated to provide appropriate ramps, elevators, unrestricted viewing areas, wheelchair turning radii, doorways and door handles, adapted bathrooms, accessible telephones, and accessible drinking fountains. "Media facilities" means that nearby parking spaces have been reserved, unrestricted viewing facilities provided, and arrangements made for access to interview/photo rooms, fax machines, phone lines for radio broadcasting, appropriate lighting for television, and computer terminals with modems.

Facilities for providing the media with pregame or half-time refreshments depend on the level of competition or the individual school's option.

Summary

To develop a successful facility maintenance plan,

1. involve all staff members and departments in assessing the need for building and service system maintenance procedures;

2. involve all staff members in developing annual maintenance plans and schedules and completing them well in advance of instructional, recreational, or competitive sport calendar dates;

3. solicit competitive bids for private maintenance contracts, with adequate lead time to ensure completion of needed projects; and

4. develop generic and site-specific checklists of equipment and facilities to simplify regular inspections by staff members.

▌ Form 5.1 — Facility Inspection List

Staff member _____

Date of inspection _____   Facility inspected _____

Check below if repairs are needed:

_____ 1. Basketball rims secure

_____ 2. Backboards protected; lifting mechanism functional

_____ 3. Bleacher supports in good repair

_____ 4. Door and door locks in good repair

_____ 5. Ductwork cleaned

_____ 6. Exit directions posted

_____ 7. Fire extinguishers in place

_____ 8. Floor condition; floor plates secure

_____ 9. Lights: overhead, scoreboard lights in good repair

_____ 10. Lockers in good repair

_____ 11. Mats clean

_____ 12. Public address system functional

_____ 13. Rest rooms functional

_____ 14. Roof leak-free

_____ 15. Scoreboard mechanism functional

_____ 16. Stairways open, lighted

_____ 17. Storage cabinets secure, functional

_____ 18. Thermostat functional

_____ 19. Timer/scorer bench in good repair

_____ 20. Walls vandalism-free

_____ 21. Wall plugs functional, covered

_____ 22. Windows secure, protected from competitive objects

_____ 23. Vent systems functional

_____ 24. Volleyball uprights padded

■ Form 5.2 — Facility Maintenance or Repair Request

Staff member _____

Date of inspection _____   Facility inspected _____

Check below if repairs are needed:

_____ 1. Basketball rims secure

_____ 2. Backboards protected; lifting mechanism functional

_____ 3. Bleacher supports in good repair

_____ 4. Door and door locks in good repair

_____ 5. Ductwork cleaned

_____ 6. Exit directions posted

_____ 7. Fire extinguishers in place

_____ 8. Floor condition; floor plates secure

_____ 9. Lights: overhead, scoreboard lights in good repair

_____ 10. Lockers in good repair

_____ 11. Mats clean

_____ 12. Public address system functional

_____ 13. Rest rooms functional

_____ 14. Roof leak-free

_____ 15. Scoreboard mechanism functional

_____ 16. Stairways open, lighted

_____ 17. Storage cabinets secure, functional

_____ 18. Thermostat functional

_____ 19. Timer/scorer bench in good repair

_____ 20. Walls vandalism-free

_____ 21. Wall plugs functional, covered

_____ 22. Windows secure, protected from competitive objects

_____ 23. Vent systems functional

_____ 24. Volleyball uprights padded

▌ Form 5.3 — Facility Maintenance Evaluation

1. Competitive activities are disrupted because of maintenance deficiencies.	Yes	No
2. Competitors are unsafe because of maintenance deficiencies.	Yes	No
3. Spectators are uncomfortable because of maintenance deficiencies.	Yes	No
4. Recreational activities are disrupted because of maintenance deficiencies.	Yes	No
5. Recreational participants are uncomfortable because of maintenance deficiencies.	Yes	No
6. Recreational participants are unsafe because of maintenance deficiencies.	Yes	No
7. Instruction is disrupted because of maintenance deficiencies.	Yes	No
8. Students are uncomfortable because of maintenance deficiencies.	Yes	No
9. Students are unsafe because of maintenance deficiencies.	Yes	No

▌ Form 5.4 — Maintenance Checklist for Aerobics

Assess the cleanliness, functionality, and need for maintenance with respect to each of the following facilities or pieces of equipment.

	Clean	Functional	Maintenance needed
ADA access			
Floor clean and safe			
Media facilities			
Music and tape player			
Public address system			
Step (exercise stairs)			
Ticket collection			
Ticket sales			

▌ Form 5.5 — Maintenance Checklist for Archery

Assess the cleanliness, functionality, and need for maintenance with respect to each of the following facilities or pieces of equipment.

	Clean	Functional	Maintenance needed
ADA access			
Bleachers			
Canvas backdrops			
Chairs for officials and competitors			
Concession stand			
Ground quivers			
Lighting			
Media facilities			
Music and tape player			
Public address system			
Security zones			
Targets			
Target stands			

▌ Form 5.6 — Maintenance Checklist for Badminton

Assess the cleanliness, functionality, and need for maintenance with respect to each of the following facilities or pieces of equipment.

	Clean	Functional	Maintenance needed
ADA access			
Birds (extra)			
Bleachers			
Competitive nets and standards			
Competitors' chairs			
Concession stand			
Floors clean and safe			
Line judge chair			
Media facilities			
Net judge chair			
Racquets (extra)			
Towels			

■ Form 5.7 — Maintenance Checklist for Baseball and Softball

Assess the cleanliness, functionality, and need for maintenance with respect to each of the following facilities or pieces of equipment.

	Clean	Functional	Maintenance needed
ADA access			
Baseballs/softballs (extra)			
Baselines in place			
Bases			
Bats			
Benches			
Bleachers			
Concession stand			
Dugout clean			
Lights operational			
Mats on outfield fences			
Music and tape player			
Plate in good repair			
Protective screen in good repair			
Public address system			
Safety zones			
Scorer table			
Ticket collection			
Ticket sales			

▌Form 5.8 — Maintenance Checklist for Basketball

Assess the cleanliness, functionality, and need for maintenance with respect to each of the following facilities or pieces of equipment.

	Clean	Functional	Maintenance needed
ADA access			
Backboards in place, padded (extra available)			
Basketballs (extra)			
Basket rims stable (extra available)			
Benches clean			
Bleachers extended, in good repair, walkways marked, railings in place			
Chairs (players', coaches')			
Concession stand			
Entry gate security			
Floors clean			
Goal nets in good repair			
Lights			
Mats in place on end walls			
Music and tape player			
Public address system			
Scoreboard and timer			
Scorer/timer table and chairs/benches			
Ticket collection			
Ticket sales			

▮ Form 5.9 — Maintenance Checklist for Bowling

Assess the cleanliness, functionality, and need for maintenance with respect to each of the following facilities or pieces of equipment.

	Clean	Functional	Maintenance needed
ADA access			
Alleys clean			
Chalk available			
Competitor seating			
Concession stand			
Hand towels			
Lighting			
Media facilities			
Public address system			
Scoring mechanism and overhead projection capability			
Spectator seating			

▮ Form 5.10 — Maintenance Checklist for Cross-Country

Assess the cleanliness, functionality, and need for maintenance with respect to each of the following facilities or pieces of equipment.

	Clean	Functional	Maintenance needed
ADA access			
Bleachers (finish area)			
Concession stand			
Cones (turns, out-of-bounds areas)			
Finish chute (finish posts, lines, flags, finish twine)			
Media facilities			
Markers (cones)			
Public address system			
Timing device			

▮ Form 5.11 — Maintenance Checklist for Crew (Rowing)

Assess the cleanliness, functionality, and need for maintenance with respect to each of the following facilities or pieces of equipment.

	Clean	Functional	Maintenance needed
ADA access			
Course security (notice to mariners)			
Bleachers			
Buoys (start, finish, course markers)			
Concession stand			
Finish line judges' stand			
Pier area clear of equipment			
Public address system			
Shells and oars ready			

▮ Form 5.12 — Maintenance Checklist for Dance

Assess the cleanliness, functionality, and need for maintenance with respect to each of the following facilities or pieces of equipment.

	Clean	Functional	Maintenance needed
ADA access			
Bleachers			
Chairs for judges			
Concession stand			
Floor clean, safe			
Lights			
Music and tape player			
Public address system			
Security			
Ticket collection			
Ticket sales			

▌Form 5.13 — Maintenance Checklist for Fencing

Assess the cleanliness, functionality, and need for maintenance with respect to each of the following facilities or pieces of equipment.

	Clean	Functional	Maintenance needed
ADA access			
Benches for competitors			
Bleachers			
Chairs for judges			
Course security			
Electrical contacts for competitors			
Floor clean and safe			
Mats, competitive			
Music and tape player			
Public address system			
Safety zone for spectators			
Scorer's table			
Ticket collection			
Ticket sales			
Weapons (extra épées, foils, sabers)			

▌Form 5.14 — Maintenance Checklist for Football

Assess the cleanliness, functionality, and need for maintenance with respect to each of the following facilities or pieces of equipment.

	Clean	Functional	Maintenance needed
ADA access			
Benches			
Bleachers			
Concession stand			
Down box and chain			
Field markings			
Flags, corner			
Footballs (extra)			
Lights			
Media facilities			
Music and tape player			
Security			
Sideline crew uniforms			
Sideline security			
Sideline yard markers			
Ticket collection			
Ticket sales			
Towels			

▌ Form 5.15 — Maintenance Checklist for Golf

Assess the cleanliness, functionality, and need for maintenance with respect to each of the following facilities or pieces of equipment.

	Clean	Functional	Maintenance needed
ADA access			
Concession stand			
Course security and rangers			
Flags			
Leader board			
Media facilities			
Score cards			
Ticket collection			
Ticket sales			

▌ Form 5.16 — Maintenance Checklist for Gymnastics

Assess the cleanliness, functionality, and need for maintenance with respect to each of the following facilities or pieces of equipment.

	Clean	Functional	Maintenance needed
ADA access			
Apparatus, floor plates, and cables in good repair			
Benches			
Bleachers			
Chairs for judges			
Chalk			
Concession stand			
Landing mats and pads in good repair			
Lights			
Media facilities			
Security			
Scorer table and chair			
Ticket collection			
Ticket sales			

Form 5.17 — Maintenance Checklist for Handball and Racquetball

Assess the cleanliness, functionality, and need for maintenance with respect to each of the following facilities or pieces of equipment.

	Clean	Functional	Maintenance needed
ADA access			
Bleachers			
Concession stand			
Floor clean			
Handballs/racquetballs (extra)			
Lights			
Public address system			

Form 5.18 — Maintenance Checklist for Hockey

Assess the cleanliness, functionality, and need for maintenance with respect to each of the following facilities or pieces of equipment.

	Clean	Functional	Maintenance needed
ADA access			
Benches			
Benches/par boxes and access doors (penalty, player) in good repair, clean			
Chairs (timer, scorer)			
Concession stand			
Goals and nets and goal lights			
Ice-cleaning machine			
Ice compressor			
Public address system			
Pucks (extra)			
Scoreboard and penalty timer			
Security			
Ticket collection			
Ticket sales			

▌Form 5.19 — Maintenance Checklist for Rugby

Assess the cleanliness, functionality, and need for maintenance with respect to each of the following facilities or pieces of equipment.

	Clean	Functional	Maintenance needed
ADA access			
Benches			
Bleachers			
Concession stand			
Field markings			
Goals			
Lights			
Media access			
Rugby balls (extra)			
Scoreboard/timer			
Security			
Ticket collection			
Ticket sales			
Towels			

Form 5.20 — Maintenance Checklist for Soccer

Assess the cleanliness, functionality, and need for maintenance with respect to each of the following facilities or pieces of equipment.

	Clean	Functional	Maintenance needed
ADA access			
Benches			
Bleachers			
Concession stand			
Field markings			
Goals and nets			
Lights			
Media facilities			
Public address system			
Scoreboard/timer			
Security			
Soccer balls (extra)			
Ticket collection			
Ticket sales			
Towels			

▌ Form 5.21 — Maintenance Checklist for Swimming and Diving

Assess the cleanliness, functionality, and need for maintenance with respect to each of the following facilities or pieces of equipment.

	Clean	Functional	Maintenance needed
ADA access			
Benches			
Chairs			
Concession stand			
Electronic lane timer			
Lane lines			
Public address system			
Security			
Ticket collection			
Ticket sales			

▌ Form 5.22 — Maintenance Checklist for Trainer Supplies

Assess the cleanliness, functionality, and need for maintenance with respect to each of the following facilities or pieces of equipment.

	Clean	Functional	Maintenance needed
(Should be available at all contests)			
Ace bandages			
Adhesive tape			
Alcohol			
Antiseptic			
Bandages			
Blood cleaning kit			
CPR mask (trainer's personal mask)			
Emergency numbers and player medical information			
Gauze			

	Clean	Functional	Maintenance needed
Hazardous material disposal bags or containers (marked Bio-hazard)			
Ice cups or other cold therapy capability			
Latex gloves			
Lubricant			
Moleskin			
Scissors			
Tape cutters			
Underwrap			

▐ Form 5.23 — Maintenance Checklist for Volleyball

Assess the cleanliness, functionality, and need for maintenance with respect to each of the following facilities or pieces of equipment.

	Clean	Functional	Maintenance needed
ADA access			
Benches			
Bleachers			
Cables marked and in good repair			
Chairs			
Concession stand			
Floor plates anchored securely			
Media facilities			
Officials' stand			
Public address system			
Scoreboard/timing mechanism			
Scorer/timer table and chairs/benches			
Ticket collection			
Ticket sales			

▌Form 5.24 — Maintenance Checklist for Wrestling

Assess the cleanliness, functionality, and need for maintenance with respect to each of the following facilities or pieces of equipment.

	Clean	Functional	Maintenance needed
ADA access			
Benches			
Bleachers			
Chairs			
Floor clean and cleared of other sport equipment			
Mats taped and anchored			
Media access			
Public address system			
Scorer/timer table and chairs/ benches			
Scoring/timing mechanism			
Ticket collection			
Ticket sales			

Chapter 6
Managing Facilities: Supervision

The task of supervising sport facilities and activity programs requires attention to numerous management details and a continuing emphasis on safety and order. The fact that most school injuries occur in sport and recreational programs emphasizes the importance of these management responsibilities. High-speed competition conducted under intense conditions may cause some students to participate with reduced judgment and unacceptable behaviors. This is precisely where you and your staff must enter the equation. Risk management programs and consistent execution of supervisory responsibilities can prevent many accidents and injuries.

In this chapter, you will learn

1. the importance of identifying and assigning competent personnel to facility supervision,

2. the importance of identifying the facilities for which you have supervisory responsibility,

3. how to conduct thorough training and orientation programs for supervisors concerning duties and obligations in the area of risk management,

4. the relationship among supervisor training, risk reduction, and participant safety, and

5. the importance of developing policies and procedures for use of facilities by outside groups.

IDENTIFYING FACILITIES FOR WHICH YOU ARE RESPONSIBLE

Supervision within the facilities located on your campus or within the building to which you are physically assigned is an obvious responsibility for you and your staff. However, you may also find it necessary to lease or rent facilities other than those you directly supervise. While these facilities are owned by other agencies, all participants who use them have a right to expect clean, safe, and controlled facilities, regardless of the type or location of the activity site. Those who engage in conditioning activities may arrive at these remote or isolated facilities in early morning hours, during the lunch hour, or in the late afternoon or evening. Regardless of the time or date of the activities that you schedule in these facilities, you will be expected to provide competent supervision.

In some cases, fitness users may conduct their conditioning activities in isolated situations where they are vulnerable to criminal acts. It is imperative to warn those who condition on their own about personal safety and the security of valuables. Equipment in these facilities must be placed and stored to create a safe environment for conditioning athletes. You must also provide safe conditions and implement safe practices for athletes who condition and train in facilities operated by other agencies.

Supervisors can be assigned from your own staff, or employees of the rented or leased site can be contracted for supervisory duties. All assigned or contracted supervisors must have the training and qualifications needed to perform their supervisory duties. You must develop a method for reserving, renting, or leasing the extramural facility(ies) and assigning responsibility for supervision. Form 6.1 (see page 87) suggests a method for accomplishing these goals.

Coaches of track and field, hockey, gymnastics, or swim teams that use facilities operated or owned by other schools or agencies must be physically present before and during practice and competitive activities. They must also implement accepted practices to protect the safety of participants. These standards will be covered in greater detail later in this chapter.

As facility manager, you may be responsible for leasing or renting these extramural facilities. Insist that your sport and activity supervisors identify any specific hazards in them so you can negotiate repair or remedy of unsafe conditions or equipment. You or your supervisors should regularly inspect locker rooms, activity sites, equipment, and building systems. Use forms 5.4 through 5.24 as a basis for developing site-specific checklists.

IDENTIFYING SUPERVISORS

Because you must delegate the direct supervision and management of activities, facilities, and equipment, you need to invest quality time and effort in identifying competent supervisors and developing focused training and orientation programs.

Supervisors should be selected for their knowledge of the fundamentals and instructional techniques of an activity and for their ability to teach these skills effectively. Their teaching methods should move from

- simple to complex skills.

- known to unknown concepts.

- individual skills to integrated, multiskill patterns.

They should also be able to teach or demonstrate the use of equipment items and to identify and stop hazardous activity within all programs under their supervision. Moreover, they should have an emergency response plan, including their own ability to implement approved responses to injuries ranging from simple to life-threatening. Clearly stated safety policies and procedures and focused management techniques can help reduce the incidence of accident and injury. Regardless of the time of day or the type of user group, supervisors must be assigned and supervisory policies instituted in all facilities for which you have responsibility.

Although certain liability reduction principles should be consistently applied in every facility, the type of facility and the age and maturity of the user population will direct your method of supervision. As a general rule, the younger or less experienced the users, the greater your responsibility as a supervisor to control behaviors and to assess the safety of the facility. Courts have ruled that children should be removed from harm's way or that dangerous facilities should be immediately repaired or closed to prevent injury or loss.

Supervision Liability?

You rent an ice arena for your high school hockey team to use for practices and competitions. The facility is located in a remote area of the city and competitions are scheduled on school nights, so it is difficult to recruit spectator supervisors even though they are paid for their supervisory services. What are the main factors you need to consider with respect to liability, public relations, spectator sportsmanship, and customer enjoyment of the hockey competition?

TRAINING SUPERVISORS

Although candidates for supervision of activity programs usually have competitive or recreational backgrounds and the motivation to serve as supervisors, they still need a through orientation and training program. This program should be site-specific and should focus on the following.

1. General policies

   - Supervision requirements
   - Security requirements
   - Interaction with other staff and administrative personnel

2. Safety procedures

   - Appropriate activities for age and development of participants
   - Management of participants' behavior
   - Facility and equipment inspections

3. Medical procedures

   - Location of the first-aid kit, spine board, and trainer's office
   - Responsibility for inspecting and restocking the first-aid kit
   - Policies for use of rehabilitative equipment

4. Emergency procedures

   - Approved procedures
   - Current emergency certification for all supervisors
   - Specific procedures for each facility

5. Accident reporting

   - Forms
   - Filing of accurate, timely reports
   - Records maintenance and storage

6. Location of facilities and procedures for issuing and returning equipment

Nonfaculty Coach

The girls gymnastics coach at your high school is employed outside the school as an insurance agent. The coach arrives at school at approximately 3:15 P.M. each day so that she can begin practice at 3:45 P.M. Prior to the coach's arrival, senior gymnasts conduct a hazing initiation in the girls locker room and shower area. In the process, one of the younger gymnasts is injured. Following an investigation of the situation, it is determined that there was no malicious act involved in the injury and that the unfortunate circumstance evolved from the thoughtless actions of a few students. To what extent might you be alleged negligent? To what extent is the coach negligent? What are your future options and requirements?

SCHEDULING SUPERVISORS

The practice of scheduling supervisors must reflect both the competence of the individual and the readiness of the participants. This may require pairing less experienced employees with more seasoned supervisors to ensure competent implementation of safety policies and instructional procedures. In other cases, special expertise may be required to supervise activities such as gymnastics, swimming, weight training, wrestling, and hockey.

A supervision schedule should be posted several days before the date when supervisors are expected to work. If students are involved in the supervisory task, you may wish to implement an acknowledgment procedure by which supervisors indicate acceptance of their assignment for the upcoming week. Figure 6.1 is a sample assignment chart.

All supervisors should arrive at least 15 minutes before their assigned supervision period to make sure equipment is available and properly set up. Reporting supervisors should check with the offgoing supervisor concerning any special situations. They must also know the location of the first-aid kit and emergency telephone. The last assigned supervisor of the evening must make sure the facility

has been vacated by all participants, turn off the lights, and lock the door securely.

DETERMINING POLICY: TEN LEGAL DUTIES

Supervisors or managers have ten legal duties. These are moral mandates in the eyes of the law and thus become not only your obligation as the facility or program manager but also the obligation of each activity director under your supervision. The following sections elaborate each of the ten duties in terms of specific supervisory responsibilities expected of you and your staff.

Duty 1: Plan Properly

Ensure that coaches and instructors are properly qualified. Develop plans to ensure that instruction, activities, and practices are appropriate for the age, physical condition, and maturity of participants. Plan for emergencies by ensuring that emergency procedures are in place. Plan for adverse weather conditions, environmental conditions, and equipment conditions.

Duty 2: Supervise Properly

It is a widely held expectation that supervision will be provided in all activity sites and generally in related areas, including locker rooms and transportation. Supervisors are expected to be competent to control the unthinking actions of participants, to assess whether the facility and participants' actions are hazardous, and to take appropriate protective action. As a facility manager or program director, you are also responsible for ensuring that activity supervisors are fully implementing risk reduction procedures during various sport activities. To fulfill this duty, you will need to visit and observe programs periodically.

Duty 3: Teach Properly

Once assigned and properly located to conduct teaching or coaching duties, a coach/supervisor is expected to teach in a logical and accepted progression

Sample Facility Supervision Assignment—Week of January 21, 1997			
Facility	6:30–7:45 A.M.	4:00–7:00 P.M.	7:00–10:00 P.M.
Gym 1	T. Smith	M. Johnson	W. Jones
Gym 2	R. Jackson	R. Lombardo	G. Hauge
Pool	T. Ritchie	G. Schmidt	C. Plautz
Weight room	S. Moss	J. Spenser	D. Marx
Dance studio	B. Emshoff	L. Thomas	D. Olson

Figure 6.1 Sample facility supervision assignment.

that leads sequentially to higher levels of knowledge, skill, and physical conditioning. Coaches should assess, instruct, and monitor athletes to help them move gradually from current levels of knowledge, skill, and conditioning to higher levels.

Supervisors are expected to be knowledgeable about the scientific bases of conditioning and the dangers inherent in sport-specific practices, equipment, or environmental conditions. They should be able to assist athlete/learners in designing practice regimens. A special application of the principle of proper teaching involves spotting for gymnastic activities that involve inverted positioning of the body and movement of the athlete through space. As the facility manager, you must require supervisors to develop instructional or practice plans that are appropriate for the age and maturity of the participants.

Duty 4: Provide a Safe Environment

This responsibility implies that supervisors and managers have the capacity to use equipment safely and to inspect, maintain, and replace it on a regular basis to ensure user satisfaction and safety. To achieve this goal, activity supervisors should be trained to recognize defective and dangerous equipment and be required to conduct regular inspections of equipment and facilities with site-specific checklists. Deficient equipment should be immediately reported to maintenance personnel and should be removed from service until it is repaired.

Duty 5: Provide Safe Equipment

Supervisors and managers must be able to use equipment safely and to inspect, maintain, and replace it

on a regular basis to ensure customer satisfaction and safety. Moreover, participants have come to expect that a trained professional (coach/supervisor) will recognize defective and dangerous equipment and remove it from program use. To achieve this goal, activity supervisors should be required to conduct regular inspections of equipment and facilities with site-specific checklists. Problems should be reported to maintenance personnel immediately and defective equipment should be removed from service until it is repaired or replaced.

Duty 6: Provide Safe Activity

Facility and activity supervisors must ensure that participants are paired appropriately based on size, age, maturity, and experience. It is particularly important to apply this principle when teaching or coaching contact sports. Activities must also be appropriate for the age and experience of the participants and for the size and configuration of the activity site. Practice or instructional plans should be appropriate for the readiness of the learners/participants. You should periodically observe all activities.

Duty 7: Warn Participants of Potential Injury

All participants should be warned of potential harm inherent within an activity. This is especially true when a particular sport technique is potentially dangerous. Moreover, interscholastic and intercollegiate athletes should be thoroughly oriented to sport-specific activities that are hazardous. For minors, it is wise to provide a statement citing sport-specific hazards to athletes and parents. This statement should be signed by both parent and athlete to certify their comprehension. Activity supervisors should keep the comprehension statements until the end of the session, semester, or season.

Duty 8: Provide Emergency Care in Case of Injury

You must ensure that activity supervisors know how to use approved first-aid techniques, especially in life-threatening conditions. Supervisors must be competent to recognize life-threatening conditions and respond appropriately. All activity supervisors should have a current certification in American Red Cross standard first aid and cardiopulmonary resuscitation.

Duty 9: Design and Implement an Emergency Response Plan

As the senior facility manager, you must develop an emergency plan for each activity site within the facility. This is especially true for remote areas that may not have good access to telephones or where stairways and exit doors make the activity site difficult to locate. These plans should be run through at least once at the start of a season or activity and should involve all supervisors or coaches who will play a role.

Duty 10: Select, Train, and Supervise Coaches, Instructors, and Supervisors

In the event of a serious injury to a facility user, you and your staff members may be legally challenged to demonstrate that you hired staff supervisors, coaches, or instructional personnel who used their specialized knowledge and skill to control the actions of activity participants and who were able to recognize and correct dangerous conditions or activities. Your employees may also be required to demonstrate that dangerous equipment was repaired

or removed and that they taught skills and knowledge properly and conditioned athletes scientifically.

You may be sued if there is an indication that you failed to provide proper training or orientation to supervisors concerning their duties and that this lack of training was related to a participant injury or loss. You should thus develop, maintain, update, and annually present a site-specific curriculum for new activity supervisors.

MONITORING SUPERVISORS

Because your activity supervisors operate with relative independence, a mechanism for monitoring the quality of their performance is important. Form 6.2 (see page 88) is a checklist of supervisory duties that you should require coaches, instructors, and managers to complete regularly.

FACILITY AND EQUIPMENT CONDITIONS

You must also ensure that your supervisors are involved in ongoing inspections of facilities and equipment conditions so that unsafe conditions can be corrected immediately. The more minor maintenance and repair problems you resolve during the school year, the more likely it is that maintenance specialists will be free for major repairs during vacation periods.

All personnel with management or supervisory responsibility must immediately report damage to facilities or equipment when discovered. The defective item or facility should be repaired immediately or taken out of service until it is repaired or replaced. A site-specific form can be used as shown in forms 3.2 and 3.3 (see pages 37 and 38) or as a component of a facility usage permit (see form 7.3 on page 101).

Form 6.3 (see page 89) is a checklist supervisors can use to inspect the equipment and activity sites in your facilities.

Who's at Fault?

Physical education teachers, athletic coaches, recreation users, and private sector program participants all make use of your resistance strength-training facility. During a private sector conditioning session, a participant is injured when a weight machine cable breaks and a weight stack falls on him. There are several user groups and supervisors who make use of the facility, so who is likely to be the focus of a lawsuit? Will you be named? Is there a designated weight room supervisor? Should there be one?

Medical Procedures

Athletic and recreational activities are administered primarily by educational institutions in the United States. Parents and taxpayers have come to believe that all sport supervisors will conduct their activities in the best interest of participants in all areas, including medical supervision. You will need to monitor the degree to which your program supervisors meet medical duties and responsibilities. Form 6.4 (see page 90) provides a monitoring instrument for this purpose.

Accident Reporting

It is important that you and members of your staff maintain an accurate record of accidents and injuries. Seek guidance from your legal counsel and insurance carrier regarding how long these records should be maintained following an incident. They are important in order to identify

1. trends in accidents and injuries,
2. injuries specific to various activities,
3. injuries specific to various facilities,

4. injuries specific to various equipment items, and
5. a need for budgetary support of maintenance and repair projects.

Form 6.5 (see page 90) suggests a method for gathering important information related to an accident or injury.

EVALUATING YOUR SUPERVISION PLAN

Your supervision plan will provide your staff with a wide range of monitoring tools that will allow them to assess the condition of facilities and equipment and the level of customer satisfaction. This information should be tabulated and analyzed regularly to determine whether

a. dangerous conditions exist (forms 6.2 through 6.5).

b. wasteful conditions exist.

c. customer dissatisfaction with facilities exists in any significant proportion (form 5.3).

d. customer dissatisfaction with equipment exists in any significant proportion (form 5.3).

e. maintenance and new purchases are meeting the needs of participants.

Areas of dissatisfaction should be addressed with a focused plan for improvement that allocates funding in proportion to

1. the degree of danger that must be controlled,
2. the number of participants who have reported dissatisfaction,
3. the costs of facility improvement or renovation, and
4. the costs of equipment repair or replacement.

Throughout this evaluation, you should carefully consider whether all factors relate to the philosophy of the institution.

Summary

To fulfill your supervisory duties for the facilities in your program,

1. recruit, hire, train, and supervise qualified activity managers;

2. orient supervisors to their legal duties and responsibilities and to conducting activities safely and in good order;

3. identify the sites within and outside your school facility for which you and your staff have supervisory and emergency responsibilities;

4. schedule facilities operated by other agencies and execute appropriate rental agreements;

5. involve all staff in identifying needed maintenance, repair, and safety improvements at these sites;

6. involve participants in identifying program, equipment, and facility deficiencies; and

7. continuously evaluate all aspects of your supervision program.

▌Form 6.1 — Facility Access Contract

The _____ requests access to the _____
          (Agency)   (Facility)

owned and operated by the Jefferson City Parks Dept. and located at 1400 E. Johnson St., Jefferson City, on the following dates:

	Dates	Times	Number of participants	Number of spectators
1.				
2.				
3.				
4.				
5.				
6.				
7.				
8.				
9.				
10.				

Supervision

Activity and spectator supervision is required for all events conducted within Parks Dept. Facilities. Please indicate in the following section how supervision will be accomplished.

The _____ will assign staff members to conduct
activities.   Yes   No

The _____ will assign staff members to supervise
spectators.   Yes   No

The _____ will contract with the Jefferson City
Parks Dept. at a rate of $ _____ per hour per supervisor.   Yes   No

The _____ will contract with the Jefferson City
Parks Dept. at a rate of $ _____ per hour per supervisor.   Yes   No

▮ Form 6.2 — Management and Supervision Checklist for Coaches, Instructors, and Managers

Indicate whether you consistently carry out the following legal responsibilities in your supervisory assignment. Do you

	Yes	No
1. maintain order and control at the activity site, in the locker room, and in hallways and outdoor access ways leading to the activity site?	___	___
2. control the unthinking behaviors of participants, even though exhibited in a competitive environment?	___	___
3. teach competitive skills with accepted instructional progressions?	___	___
4. recognize dangerous conditions within the facilities you supervise?	___	___
5. administer accepted emergency responses for injuries?	___	___
6. have a site-specific emergency response plan?	___	___
7. disallow entry to the facility by unauthorized participants?	___	___
8. control the numbers of athletes within a facility?	___	___
9. pair young athletes comparably by weight, maturity, and experience?	___	___
10. supervise the fitting of protective equipment by qualified personnel?	___	___
11. require students to wear protective equipment properly?	___	___
12. keep alert to severe weather conditions?	___	___
13. issue or post sport-specific warning statements for athletes?	___	___
14. require written acknowledgment of sport hazards through a comprehension statement signed by the athlete and parent?	___	___

▋ Form 6.3 — Supervision Checklist

Have you checked

	Yes	No
1. all weight-bearing and gymnastics apparatus for		
a. worn leather and splintered handle grips on vaulting/side horses?	___	___
b. splintered or worn parallel rails?	___	___
c. adequate thickness and shock-absorption capability of crash mats?	___	___
d. effective location of crash mats for dismounting or somersaulting activity?	___	___
2. outdoor facilities for broken glass, ruts, and woody plants in play areas?	___	___
3. wall or floor mats to cover equipment that protrudes within the activity space?	___	___
4. all weight machine cables and pulleys for wear?	___	___
5. for nonskid material on weight machine footpedals?	___	___
6. weight benches for stability and strength?	___	___
7. weight bar collars and hardware for rusting and stripped threads on fastening apparatus?	___	___
8. stability of all floor plates used to secure gymnastics equipment or net standards for volleyball or badminton?	___	___
9. condition of nonskid material on diving boards?	___	___
10. welds on the diving-board platform and fulcrum?	___	___
11. condition of nonskid material on locker room floors and shower areas?	___	___
12. properly grounded plugs and outlets in locker rooms, shower areas, pool areas, and training rooms?	___	___
13. the availability of proper rescue and emergency equipment to all facilities?	___	___

▮ Form 6.4 — Medical Procedures

Are the following procedures consistently implemented?

	Yes	No
1. All athletes have a physical examination as required by the state high school athletic association or collegiate association.	____	____
2. Injured participants do not practice until cleared by a physician.	____	____
3. Supervisors do not prescribe long-term treatments for injuries.	____	____
4. Supervisors administer approved first aid when required.	____	____
5. Emergency response procedures are defined for each facility.	____	____
6. Medically approved conditioning sequences are used.	____	____
7. Players who display a lack of general awareness, shock, or physical or emotional distress are not released unless arrangements have been made for adult supervision and transportation.	____	____
8. A plan for preventing transmission of blood-borne pathogens has been disseminated to all coaches and supervisors.	____	____

▮ Form 6.5 — Accident Report Form

_____	_____	____/____	_____	_____
Injured's name	Identification number	Age/grade	Address	Telephone

Rescue vehicle called	Yes No	Administrator called	Yes No
Police called	Yes No	Parent notified	Yes No
School nurse called	Yes No	Family physician called	Yes No

Describe in detail the events that led to or caused the accident and/or injury(ies) and the actions taken following the incident.

_____	_____	_____
Supervisor at the time of the incident	Facility supervisor	Safety supervisor

Chapter 7

Managing Facilities: Scheduling

Coordinating schedules for the various user groups that require access to the sport facilities for which you are responsible can elicit responses that range from great enthusiasm to deep frustration. For this reason, it is important to take guidance and direction in the scheduling process from a clearly articulated philosophical rationale that has been approved by the leadership of your institution.

Since your facilities are highly sought after by instructors, coaches, other extracurricular leaders, and private-sector users, your scheduling procedures must stand a three-part test of logic, equity, and customer responsiveness.

Whether assigned as athletic director, physical education chair, or recreation supervisor, you will find the task of scheduling facilities an ongoing challenge. Access to activity sites will be expected by the general student population (and their parents) and will be heavily requested by sport, recreation, drama, or music groups. Various citizen organizations will also request access to these facilities for a wide variety of purposes.

In determining priorities for access, you will need to be guided by key principles.

1. The institutional philosophy
2. Equity and inclusion laws
   - Title IX
   - The Americans With Disabilities Act
3. The primary mission of the school or facility
   - instruction
   - recreation
   - athletics
4. The types and sizes of gyms and other sites within or adjacent to the facility

In this chapter, you will learn

1. a rationale for scheduling facilities,
2. the need for coordinated scheduling procedures,
3. procedures for scheduling off-campus facilities,
4. the priorities of legal mandates and community traditions in scheduling, and
5. how to evaluate your facility scheduling plan.

IDENTIFYING FACILITIES FOR WHICH YOU ARE RESPONSIBLE

To acquire an overview of potential and actual demands for schedule access to the facilities under your supervision, you and your staff members may wish to develop a scheduling matrix that correlates all available activity sites to recent requests for access by various user groups. This mechanism allows you to focus on past usage patterns and previous conflicts in requests for access. It can also reveal past conflicts during the transition between seasons or among instructional, athletic, and recreational activities. And it allows you to identify past schedule problems that occurred during maintenance, cleaning, and renovation periods.

Figure 7.1 illustrates the use of this scheduling tool. Representatives of each department should list their planned activities under the proper month columns to pinpoint activity conflicts and decide whether they can resolve these conflicts by altering the dates or whether alternative facilities are available.

DETERMINING FACILITY NEEDS

Now that you are aware of past schedule conflicts, you are ready to allow members of the instructional, coaching, and recreational staff an opportunity to request facility access within a calendar that reflects their instructional units or competitive or recreational seasons. You may wish to resolve schedule conflicts by publishing guidelines for scheduling that reflect the institutional philosophy. Or you could meet with those supervisors whose schedule requests conflict in order to develop facility rotation plans.

You will also need to integrate maintenance plans, budgeting, and equipment ordering that coordinate with the needs of the activity programs. Form 7.1 (see page 99) is a facility request form for staff members to use when scheduling activities for the upcoming school year. Note that more than one activity can be scheduled. This form should be used in conjunction with figure 7.1 to identify potential conflicts during the calendar year.

When facility access requests have been coordinated with maintenance and logistics schedules, you can confirm your supervisors' requests with enough lead time that they can plan their competitive seasons and instructional or recreational calendars. This is especially important if you plan to rotate practice

Scheduling Matrix												
Requesting agency	**Aug**	**Sep**	**Oct**	**Nov**	**Dec**	**Jan**	**Feb**	**Mar**	**Apr**	**May**	**Jun**	**Jul**
Required physical education												
Elective physical education												
Intramurals												
Recreation												
Athletics												
Private-sector rentals												

Figure 7.1 Scheduling matrix.

or competitive dates and times to avoid schedule conflicts.

INSTITUTIONAL PHILOSOPHY AND SCHEDULING

A school or university that values and supports high-quality physical education programs as an extension of its institutional philosophy will not give noninstructional users much access to facilities between 7:45 A.M. and 4:00 P.M. An exception may be during the noon recess period, when recreational or conditioning users may be allowed in.

However, this joint usage pattern will undoubtedly require rapid conversion of all gyms and equipment from instructional to recreational use and restoration in time for afternoon classes. In a high school setting, custodians may be busy with cafeteria or building cleaning responsibilities. In a collegiate environment, they may be responsible for general site maintenance or building management. So thoughtful assignment and involvement of staff members is needed to rapidly move large equipment; set up chairs, nets, and standards; raise or lower backboards; and store or set up small equipment, such as racquets, birds, tennis balls, golf balls and clubs, or archery equipment.

Figure 7.2 illustrates the complexity of this scheduling challenge. The key in figure 7.2 shows the types of equipment or facility changes needed. This model assumes equity for athletes of both genders and access by disabled participants.

In a physical plant facility built primarily for athletic practices and competition, instructional units may receive a lower priority, as illustrated in figure 7.3. Note that here physical education classes have been assigned five or six hours per day, while campus recreational activities have access in the early morning and from 7:00 to 10:00 P.M. Note also that athletic practices are scheduled during midday hours, which are traditionally reserved for instructional or recreational users. In addition, sport teams are assigned a 4.5-hour practice block beginning at 2:30 P.M.

NONSCHOOL USERS AND PRIVATE RENTALS

In some communities, you may be expected to reserve blocks of time for access by community organizations. Included are youth service agencies (such as scouts), religious groups, music organizations, community fund-raisers, intramurals, and high school classes holding meetings. Instructional units

Facility and Equipment Rotation Plan for Instructional Facilities

Class time	Gym 1	Gym 2	Pool	Weight room	Dance studio
7:45 A.M.	[A]Basketball 1	[C]Volleyball	[F]Lifesaving	[I]Conditioning 1	[K]Modern 1
8:50 A.M.	[A]Basketball 1	[C]Volleyball	[G]Basic swim	[I]Conditioning 1	[K]Modern 1
9:55 A.M.	[B]Badminton	[B]Badminton	[F]Basic swim	[I]Conditioning 1	[K]Ballet 2
11:00 A.M.	[B]Badminton	[B]Badminton	[H]Scuba	[I]Conditioning 2	[K]Ballet 2
11:50 A.M.	[A]Jogging	[A]3-person basketball	[F]Lap swim	[I]Open lifting	[L]Step aerobics
1:20 P.M.	[A]Basketball 2	[C]Volleyball	[F]Lifesaving	[J]Body building	[K]Interpretive dance
2:25 P.M.	[A]Basketball 2	[E]Adaptive sport	[G]Basic swim	[C]Conditioning 2	[K]Modern 1
3:30 P.M. Athletics	[C]Boys' volleyball	[C]Girls' volleyball	[F]Boys' swim team	[I]Winter conditioning	[L]Dance club
6:45 P.M. Recreation	[A]Recreational basketball	[C]Recreational volleyball	[G]Free swim	[J]Weight training	[L]Dance club

Equipment/facility key

A. Backboards down, basketballs (scoreboard)
B. Backboards up, badminton nets/poles, racquets, birds
C. Backboards up, volleyball poles, nets, volleyballs
D. Backboards up, team handballs, team handballs goals
E. Specialized adaptive PE equipment required by individualized education programs
F. Bleachers, pull buoys, poles, spine board, CPR mannequins
G. Lifeguard chair, pull buoys, lane lines in 2/3 lanes
H. All items in G plus secure storage for tanks and regulators
I. All free and machine weights, computer programs, safety belts, benches
J. Light free weights, benches
K. Lights, ventilation, appropriate music tapes, tape player, speakers
L. Aerobic dance steps plus all items in K

Figure 7.2 Facility and equipment rotation plan for instructional facilities.

are still generally scheduled as a first priority; then certain traditional dates and times are blocked out for nonschool users. After you respond to the needs of these two user groups, you can make the facility available to athletic teams or recreational users.

PROCEDURES FOR RESERVING FACILITIES

You will probably need to develop or implement a system for reserving facilities that can be used by teams and user groups under your direct supervision, other campus recreational users, and outside rental groups. Typically, permits for use of buildings and activity sites for the school year are issued beginning July 1. In multipurpose, tax-subsidized facilities, campus instructional users are generally allowed to reserve facilities first, campus intramural and recreational or athletic users second, and noncampus users last.

Physical activity sites are extremely popular, and unscheduled times will surely be rented by private-sector groups such as the scouts, musical organizations, or community groups. It is thus important that program supervisors reserve facilities for all needed

Facility and Equipment Rotation Plan for Athletic Facilities

Time	Field house	Outdoor courts	Weight room	Pool	Multipurpose gym
6:00 A.M.[###]	Recreational jogging	Recreational tennis	Winter sports conditioning	Lap swim	Step aerobics
7:45 A.M.	Basketball 1	Tennis 1	Conditioning 1	Aquacize	Adapted physical education
8:50 A.M.	Basketball 1	Tennis 1	Conditioning 2	Life guard 1	Dance 1
9:55 A.M.	Volleyball 1/2	Tennis 2	Conditioning 2	Aquacize 1	Dance 2
11:00 A.M.[***]	Team free throws	Tennis team	In-season conditioning	Swim team	Wrestling team
1:20 P.M.	Volleyball 1	Tennis 1	Conditioning 2	Aquacize	Adapted physical education
2:30 -7:00 P.M.[***]	Basketball team	Tennis team	In-season rehabilitation	Swim team	Wrestling team
7:00-10:00 P.M[###]	Campus recreation	Campus recreation	Campus recreation	Campus recreation	Campus dance club
Equipment moves	Backboards up/down	Ball-throwing machine, nets, poles	Free and machine weights of various resistances	Lane lines	Appropriate adapted equipment and mats

[***] = Periods reserved for intercollegiate athletics.
[###] = Periods reserved for college recreation programs.

Figure 7.3 Facility and equipment rotation plan for athletic facilities.

weekend, holiday, and teacher convention and in-service days.

A policy must be also be developed concerning Sunday rentals and the use of school activity sites for religious ceremonies. Some municipalities do not permit rental of school facilities for religious activities; others require them to be closed on certain evenings or religious observation dates. It may be prudent to involve community representatives in developing a philosophy that will direct the scheduling process.

Snowed Out

Your wrestling squad was scheduled to compete for the conference championship on Tuesday evening, but a snowstorm required you to reschedule the match. The wrestling coach asks that the Tuesday match be rescheduled for Wednesday evening. You inform the coach that there can

be no competition or practices on Wednesday evening because of a long-standing policy that dedicates that period of time to family and religious activities in the community. What are your options? Could this problem have been avoided?

Rental Fees and Insurance Coverage for Private Users

When facilities are rented out to private-sector user groups, you must alert them to the costs of weekend rental charges, overtime costs for custodians or maintenance personnel, and the need for insurance coverage. Private-sector users are generally not covered by the institution's or facility's liability insurance, so they must provide their own coverage for injury, loss, or damage before you can grant access. Rental and custodian overtime charges can be quite high and must be clearly specified to weekend rental or user groups.

Form 7.2 (see page 100) is a sample facility request form for school and nonschool users. Note that it requests user information and clearly spells out both the insurance requirement and the rental charges for various facilities.

Granting Access

When you have considered all facility requests, you should have a permit to give those user groups that are granted access. The facility permit guarantees them use of a designated space for specified dates and times unless circumstances arise that are beyond the control of all concerned (e.g., weather, fire, or other emergency). Form 7.3 (see page 101) illustrates this authorization document.

 # SCHEDULING ADAPTED SPORT ACTIVITIES

The goal in scheduling activities for cognitively and physically challenged individuals is providing access or inclusion in the "least restrictive" environment possible. This federal law may require you to develop a continuum of instructional services.

1. Separate, remedial classes

2. Integration of challenged students into mainstream classes supported with adapted equipment

3. Partial integration into mainstream classes with staff support

4. Full integration into mainstream classes with staff support

5. Full integration into mainstream classes without staff support

6. Competition in adapted competitive sport

7. Competition in mainstream competitive sport

These legal mandates require ongoing assessment of each student's knowledge, skill, and personal adjustment. Developmental, medical, and psychological factors may also be considered.

Facility and equipment modifications may be required to accommodate the needs of challenged individuals. Such modifications may include ramps, lifts, elevators, widened access doors, wheelchair turning radii, modified drinking fountains, and accessible toilet spaces. In addition, protective helmets, sonic equipment, special mats, and modified equipment (bats, racquets, etc.) may be needed. Ease of conversion and adequate storage are keys to flexibility in scheduling for adapted classes.

 # EQUITY CONSIDERATIONS

Gender equity in facilities and equipment has been an absolute requirement since passage of Title IX of the Education Amendments Act of 1972. This federal law covers scheduling as well as a host of other equity considerations for physical education, athletics, and recreation.

These federal laws, in conjunction with new National Collegiate Athletic Association (NCAA) regulations requiring increased participation opportunities and more athletic scholarships for female athletes, should lead to greater demand for access to facilities and a greater number of improved facilities and schedules throughout the next decade.

You will need to consider certain equity factors related to the scheduling of practice, competitive, and support facilities.

- Access to the same or equal practice sites

- Access to the same or equal competitive sites

- Access to equal locker rooms and related facilities

- Access to the same or equal strength-training facilities

- Access to the same or equal athletic training and sports medicine facilities

- Access to the same or equal film/video facilities

- Access to the same or equal counseling and advising services

The implications of this legislation become particularly acute when the number of available facilities is limited. Facility and equipment access must be rotated so that practice and competitive dates and times are equitably assigned.

 SCHEDULING ACTIVITIES AT OTHER SITES

You may need to communicate with managers or supervisors of other facilities in order to reserve space and time in these facilities and to develop rental, maintenance, and other financial arrangements. Typically, specific terms are defined by an annual contract. Additional written communications are made to request needed repairs, maintenance, or facility renovation. Examples include indoor swimming pools, ice rinks, gymnastics facilities, indoor tracks, and indoor tennis or badminton courts. The following contract specifications should be considered.

- Times and dates of practice, competition, or performance and earliest time of facility access for all dates
- Rental costs per hour or event
- Costs of facility preparation and cleaning
- Requirements and costs for security and supervision
- Requirements for assignment of contest officials, including timers, scorers, and judges
- Accountability for damage or theft
- Ticket sales responsibilities and revenue distributions from ticket sales

- Concession stand and other sales rights or profit distributions
- Procedure for requesting repairs, maintenance, or renovation and cost-sharing responsibilities

Form 7.4 (see page 102) is a rental agreement contract that specifies the terms of access and use of the facility.

 EVALUATING YOUR FACILITY SCHEDULING PLAN

How you handle scheduling of instructional, intramural, recreational, and athletic activities has a significant impact on the morale and satisfaction of participants, supervisors, and taxpayers. Your image as an effective facility manager will derive in large part from the effort you and your staff commit to creative, responsive scheduling. You should conduct regular assessments of participant satisfaction and the degree to which you are avoiding scheduling conflicts. Evaluation criteria should include scheduling effectiveness and participant satisfaction among

1. required physical education classes,
2. elective physical education classes,

3. adapted physical education classes,

4. recreational activities,

5. intramural activities,

6. athletic practices and competition,

7. commercial user groups, and

8. drama and music users.

You should also determine

1. whether scheduling reflects the institution's philosophy,

2. whether equipment can be scheduled and used for multiple programs and purposes,

3. whether equipment can quickly be moved from one area to another, and

4. whether equipment can be stored safely and securely while other groups use the facilities.

Summary

To successfully manage scheduling for your facilities, you must

1. evaluate the mission and philosophy of the institution;

2. take into consideration the traditions of the community;

3. follow equity and inclusion mandates of federal law;

4. respond to customer needs and satisfaction (as defined by regular program evaluations); and

5. make an effort to resolve conflicts on a continuing basis.

▋ Form 7.1 — Staff Facility Request Form

Staff member _____

Office phone _____   Date of request _____

Facilities requested	Dates requested	Equipment needed	Access confirmed (Office use)
1.	1.	1.	1.
2.	2.	2.	2.
3.	3.	3.	3.
4.	4.	4.	4.

▌ Form 7.2 — Facility Request Form

_____

(Name of requesting group)

requests use of the following facilities at _____

(High school)

Rental fees

Check facility desired:	Week night	Saturday	Sunday
____ Spectator gym	$ 6.00/hour	$ 9.00/hour	$12.00/hour
____ Multipurpose gym	6.00/hour	9.00/hour	12.00/hour
____ Dance lab	6.00/hour	9.00/hour	12.00/hour
____ Strength-training facility	9.00/hour	13.50/hour	18.00/hour
____ Swimming pool	20.00/hour	30.00/hour	40.00/hour

Equipment desired (instructional, officiating, recreational, audiovisual):

1.

2.

3.

4.

Name _____   Telephone _____

Address _____

_____

(Signature)

Dates requested   Times requested

1.   1.

2.   2.

3.   3.

NOTE: Private-sector facility users must provide a certificate of insurance coverage to indemnify the (School Name) for damages or loss that accrue to its users. In addition, insurance must cover the loss of equipment or damage to the facility in an amount not less than $500,000 per incident.

▌ Form 7.3 — Facility Permit

_____ is authorized use of:

_____ A. Spectator gymnasium   _____ C. Pool

_____ B. Fieldhouse court 1   _____ D. Weight room

_____ C. Fieldhouse court 2   _____ E. Multipurpose gym

on the following dates and times:

Dates	Times
1.	1.
2.	2.
3.	3.
4.	4.

Facility condition report following use:

Cleanliness ☐   Acceptable ☐   Unacceptable ☐

Vandalism ☐ Yes   ☐ No

Specify: _____

_____

_____

_____

_____

Equipment breakage ☐ Yes   ☐ No

Specify: _____

_____

_____

_____

_____

_____

_____ / _____   _____ / _____

Custodian signature/Date   Facility manager/Date

▌ Form 7.4 — Facility Rental Agreement

_____ is authorized use of the

_____

on _____ 19 ____ from _____ A.M./P.M. to _____ A.M./P.M.

These facilities shall be rented at a rate of $ _____ per hour and an additional charge
for custodial overtime of $ _____ per hour for use of the facilities after 1:00 P.M. on
Saturday and all day Sunday. An insurance certificate in the amount of $500,000 must
be returned with this signed contract. Such insurance certificate shall indemnify
the _____ against liability for injury or loss. Damage to the
     (Organization)
facility or loss of equipment will be assessed to the renting agency.

   Contest supervisors, security agents, officials, and judges will be the responsibility of
the renting agency.

_____   _____

(Facility manager)   (Organization representative)

_____   _____

(Date)   (Date)

Chapter 8
Facility Planning

Planning a new athletic, instructional, or recreational facility is an exciting and challenging task that requires dedication to detail, selection of cost-effective construction procedures and materials, and a commitment to customer satisfaction. You should be able to measure the results of this process in terms of the new programs it makes available to students, faculty, and local citizens and their satisfaction with the new facility.

The process of planning and constructing a new sport facility presents an opportunity to involve members of the community, sport supervisors, engineers, architects, and other professionals in a planning partnership aimed at achieving maximal utility, efficiency, and customer satisfaction. This is a rare chance to coordinate the efforts of diverse user groups with those of sport and construction experts in the design and planning of a facility that incorporates state-of-the-art building concepts, high-demand facilities, and modern equipment.

In this chapter, you will learn

1. an overview of various planning factors that must be accomplished before and during the construction process,

2. insights into the makeup of a facility construction planning committee,

3. factors you must consider in the facility planning and construction proposal processes,

4. considerations related to land acquisition procedures,

5. considerations related to construction bid factors, and

6. suggestions for evaluating your facility planning model.

FUNDING SOURCES

The traditional source of capital funding for construction or renovation of educational facilities has been the sale of municipal or construction bonds to investors. These bonds may yield a moderate rate of tax-exempt interest that is paid to purchasers from fiscal revenues collected from state and local taxpayers. In addition, gifts, state fiscal revenues, and tuition increases have been jointly used to fund university construction projects.

However, during periods marked by inflation, unemployment, and high interest rates, legislators have been reluctant to approve any measures that would place added burdens on taxpayers. To solve the problem, try researching the following funding sources as potential supplements to tax revenues for construction or renovation.

Research Grants

Capital funding in the form of research grants may be made available from government or private industry sources. This resource usually requires that the institution, government body, or private-sector agency match the sum and be dedicated to construction of facilities for biodynamics, cardiac rehabilitation, or other scientific research.

These facilities may include pools, gyms, or rehabilitative facilities, in addition to physiology or kinesiology research centers. Potential funding sources include the American Medical Association, the American Heart Association, the American College of Sports Medicine, pharmaceutical corporations, and the U.S. Centers for Disease Control.

Private Industry Grants

Biomedical, health insurance, and fitness equipment companies or large corporations may wish to defray their tax liability with donations of money to finance the construction of health or education projects. Citing these benefactors with commemorative plaques or cornerstones is a common recognition courtesy. Sporting goods companies, conditioning equipment manufacturers, and athletic clothing distributors may provide in-kind equipment contributions or be willing to make cash donations.

Endowments and Bequests

Endowments and bequests are funds donated directly to an institution's athletic or recreation department or indirectly through a foundation for a specific construction program. They are often the product of an estate or the benevolent outreach of a philanthropic individual or organization.

The use of these external revenues along with tax funds designated for athletic, instructional, or recreational purposes has been politically defensible for school administrators and appears to be increasingly acceptable to legislators and taxpayers as the concept of private and public-sector partnerships continues to evolve.

Developing Financial Support

Lobbyists and special interest groups should be informed of the methods that will be used to gain public support and to allocate or acquire construction funds. These interested parties should also be made aware of the timeline for decision making. Whether a governing board or a public referendum will be used to decide the economic support question, the efforts of these facilitators and supportive interest groups will be important.

Parents, students, coaches, teachers, and administrators should be encouraged to seek opportunities to support the construction concept at service club luncheons, faculty groups, neighborhood gatherings, PTA events, and education board meetings. This process may take six to 10 months and will require careful planning, persistence, intense commitment, and focused coordination.

If a public referendum will be used to decide the question of construction funding, efforts should focus on encouraging a large voter turnout among those community residents who support the concept. It is important to remember that capital funding referenda are often placed on the ballot during primary elections, which tend to have low voter participation. Strong support during these preliminary elections can be a key to success.

PRIMARY PLANNING COMMITTEE

Once economic support for construction has been assured, a primary planning committee should be formed. The primary planning committee serves to translate the needs of staff members, students, and various user groups into functional concepts that can be developed into architectural plans within the authorized funding level.

You and the members of your staff will have an opportunity to join other representatives of the teaching staff, the recreation and athletic departments, the custodial/maintenance staff, and engineering or construction specialists to develop a responsive, cost-effective plan. Legal and financial advisers may be involved as needed, and middle-level institution leaders should be sought as advisory liaisons to senior executives and the institutional governing board.

Committee members should be recruited for their personal interest and willingness to represent the needs of their respective colleagues and programs and for their informed ability to research new trends and technologies. The exact membership of this committee will be determined by the designated

purpose of the proposed facility or site. Thus, dance and choreography specialists should be included if a dance studio is to be constructed; aquatics experts should be invited to provide insights concerning pools and diving wells; and other knowledgeable recreation and athletic leaders should be recruited for their expertise in a specific area.

Two-Year Commitment

A commitment of approximately two years will be required from the time the project is authorized until all aspects of the construction process are completed. Committee membership can be a challenging responsibility for staff members who work in full-time administrative, teaching, coaching, or recreational jobs. In fairness, this factor should be explained to all personnel who are being considered for the committee. A list of potential members of your construction planning committee and their responsibilities follows.

Construction Planning Committee Responsibilities

Instructional representatives should research modern, innovative programs and facilities and architectural literature that demonstrate

—instructional square footage needed for

- team sports,
- lifetime/leisure activities,
- conditioning activities (resistive/aerobic),
- aquatic program needs,
- dance needs, and
- outdoor facility needs;

—specialized needs for adapted physical education;

—specialized locker room/shower, laundry needs;

—specialized equipment needs; and

—specialized storage needs.

Athletic representatives should bring official playing and facility dimension regulations, contemporary catalog references, and literature searches for information about

—practice and competitive area needs,

—scoreboard needs,

—timer/scorer facility and equipment needs,

—press box and media space and equipment needs,

—ticket sale/collection needs,

—spectator seating needs,

—video recording area and equipment needs,

—officials' locker room needs,

—coaches' office needs,

—male and female team room needs,

—male and female film and meeting room needs,

—male and female strength-training facilities,

—athletic trainer equipment and rehabilitation space needs, and

—athletic equipment storage needs.

Recreational representatives should develop proposals based on participant and supervisor interests and assessments of needs for

—recreational storage space,

—recreational office space,

—square footage for specialized recreational activities,

—square footage for program enrollment and processing procedures, and

—recreational program storage.

Student representatives should provide data-based student perspectives concerning contemporary interests and needs with respect to

—activity spaces,

—accessibility of the proposed facility to student and community housing, and

—preferred activity interests.

Architects should be asked to document a successful record of practical experience in the construction of activity sites with

—expertise in reading detailed engineering plans and specifications,

—expertise in interpreting institution proposals to construction firm engineers and specialists,

—competence in the interpretation of OSHA, DILHR, ADA, and local building code requirements, and

—expertise in monitoring construction accomplishments in terms of

• construction quality,

• use of materials,

• completion timelines, and

• design specifications.

Legal counsel should be retained as needed to evaluate and interpret

—contractual provisions,

—ADA requirements,

—Title IX requirements, and

—statutes concerning bidding, contracting, and finance.

Administrators should be asked to research institutional policies, directives, and regulations to ensure that planning, bidding, and contracting procedures comply with existing protocol. They should also assess the construction proposal's consistency with the institutional philosophy.

HIRING AN ARCHITECTURAL AND CONSTRUCTION CONSULTANT

The construction of sport facilities can be costly and is usually of great interest to potential users and community residents. Timelines for building and project completion must be met to establish credibility with taxpayers and investors. Once a completion date is set, long-range scheduling of instructional activities, athletic contests, recreation programs, and other activities can be conducted with confidence. To accomplish these goals, it is imperative that your committee retain the services of a competent architect or engineering consultant.

Because tax funds will be used to some extent, this expert must be involved early in the process to ensure maximum cost-effectiveness in selecting and using materials, implementing building procedures, choosing a construction firm, monitoring the progress of the project, and judging the quality of the work. This specialist will be the institution's direct liaison with the construction firm's architect. Early agreements and negotiations with construction company agents should make it clear that this individual will be continually involved as spokesperson and personal representative of the institution throughout the construction process.

Consultant Qualifications

The individual acting as the school or corporate consultant should possess the following minimum qualifications.

1. Special expertise and experience required to respond to activity program needs.

2. Understanding of the construction business and its logistical needs, construction trades personnel, and construction time requirements.

3. Ability to interpret specific program needs into materials, designs, and structures.

4. Ability to identify architectural and construction problems or deficiencies and interpret them to the planning team.

5. Ability to recognize sources of cost or time overruns and prevent them. Along with the institution's legal counsel, this individual should be directly involved in designing the penalty clause in the contract, which holds the construction firm to a designated completion date. He or she should also be able to apply contemporary management skills such as critical path and quality management planning tools.

6. Ability to understand square footage needs for athletic activities, pedestrian and vehicular traffic, storage, energy conservation, spectatorship, and other special functions.

7. Ability to review funding sources and their use throughout the project. Along with the institution's attorney, this individual should be involved in the final approval of any installment payment.

8. Ability to determine whether changes in the original construction proposal are legitimate or have potential for exceeding the bid.

9. Ability to inspect the interim stages of construction and the finished project for improper design, construction deficiencies, and defective equipment.

Selecting an Architect

One of the early duties of the planning committee may be selection of the architect who will help to develop the initial plans and make revisions, with guidance from committee members and their constituents. The architect may begin specific design proposals for review and approval by the planning committee. Over time, the architect prepares and revises plans that respond to the broadest range of users, activity supervisors, customers, and experts in the architectural and construction industries.

This system of checks, balances, and review leads to a sense of open communication and trust, which creates a favorable working atmosphere for the project duration. When a plan has been developed that is satisfactory to all planning committee members, the institution's legal counsel and business staff prepare a request for proposals (RFP), which is distributed broadly in the media and in various construction trade journals to seek bids from construction firms.

Communication Guidelines

The planning team should agree from inception on the communication guidelines and procedures to be used. Typically, when the planning team has any problems or concerns, it presents them to the architects, engineers, and consultants of the construction firm for response, resolution, or negotiation. Other planning team members should not go to the construction site to initiate discussions with tradespeople or foremen concerning needs or problems.

CONSTRUCTION SITE CONSIDERATIONS

If land was not acquired before formation of the planning committee, a building site must be identified and acquired. Of concern here are the following factors.

1. Location

   • Proximity to and disruption of adjacent neighborhood activity. Is there adequate space to accomplish the intended project? Will there be a disruptive impact on surrounding instruction or commerce?

   • Ease of access by student and community user groups. Is the site too distant, or does it present accessibility challenges?

   • Proximity to pedestrian and vehicular traffic routes. Will spectator or recreational participation be limited by physical limitations in the road, highway, bike path, or sidewalk access routes?

   • Ease of access from major highways and airports. Will spectator revenues and participation be limited by difficult access from major transportation facilities?

   • Ease of access to handicapped individuals. What special engineering considerations will be needed to comply with the ADA?

   • Potential disruption of academic programs. What will be the effect of construction activity, debris, equipment movement, and environmental contamination on classroom activity?

   • Potential for aesthetic or architectural incompatibility. Has an architectural subcommittee been convened to assess the compatibility of the new facility and grounds with existing architecture and landscaping?

2. Availability and costs

   • Protected sites (parks, ecologic areas, and historic sites). Is there potential for impact on protected lands or waterways? Will construction be constrained by state or federal limitations on building activities near these areas?

   • Environmental impact assessments. Have federal and state guidelines been met with respect to assessing the impact of construction on natural waterways, wetlands, and wildlife habitats?

   • Privately owned sites. How will adjacent properties be protected or restored if access to utilities requires excavation or earth movement and storage on them?

   • Current and projected land values. What is the cost of the adjacent property? What is the local and state trend in property valuation?

   • Liens, overdue taxes, or other encumbrances. Are there hidden debt-service costs that must be resolved with the local or state government before the adjacent property can be acquired?

3. Topographic considerations

   • Soil stratification and compatibility with excavation and footing supports. Is there an underlying stratum that promotes or deters foundation-level drainage?

   • Drainage, erosion, and seismic fault lines. Are there geologic conditions that could compromise the stability of foundation structures?

   • Ease of access to major utility sources. What problems will be involved in gaining access to adequate electric, water, and natural gas resources?

   • Need to remove underground tanks or toxic and polluted soils. A direct extension of the environmental impact assessment, this requirement adds costs to any construction project involving such excavation.

Facility Space Needs

The team's orientation should be to meet the greatest number of needs for each program that will operate within the planned facility. Each member/specialist should bring to early planning sessions specific activity needs and responsive design suggestions.

Members may address design and construction considerations by researching recent construction or renovation projects for innovative solutions or unexpected problems; soliciting opinions from the staffs of other institutions as to problems and potential solutions; consulting with various specialists in the field of athletic/recreation facility construction; and conducting computer searches of current trade and industry periodicals or publications specific to sport facilities. From these sources of information, a comprehensive, needs-oriented concept can be developed, negotiated, and resolved within the framework of Title IX, ADA, OSHA, and DILHR regulations, state building codes, and existing funds.

Program Standards and Innovations

The committee should research the following areas related to competitive standards, playing rules, and facility innovations when developing facilities designed to respond to specific program needs.

- Official court/field/track/pool dimensions and safety zones
- Required and desirable ceiling heights
- Desirable instructional, competitive, and recreational illumination standards
- Desirable background and contrast standards
- Quick conversion equipment and facilities for rapid, easy changes in activities
- Desirable and safe competitive surfaces
- Energy conservation methods
- Traffic control patterns and service area access
- Innovations in spectator comfort and sight lines
- Innovations in auxiliary sport facilities (offices, meeting rooms, large group assembly areas, and specialized facilities for counseling, instruction, tutoring, sports medicine services, and program administration)
- Innovations in electronic and print media facilities
- Ease of separation of instructional, athletic, and recreational activities
- Innovations in access to, location of, and size of storage areas

Specific Facility Considerations

A number of considerations mandate involvement of staff specialists who understand the needs of their programs and are motivated to research facility in-

novations. These experts may be able to design a prototype facility that can resolve program disruptions or reduce dangerous conditions that result from traditional construction designs. Among the facilities that should be considered are the following.

1. Spectator facilities could have enough square footage to allow simultaneous practices for men's and women's teams in volleyball or basketball.
2. Gymnastics or wrestling facilities could allow for simultaneous practice of men's and women's teams.
3. A 200-meter pool with movable bulkheads and/or floors would allow for flexible configuration for recreation, athletics, and instruction. A separate diving well may also be considered. Decisions concerning diving-board height and pool depth should reflect participant interests and safety.
4. Strength-training facilities equipped with a wide range of exercise equipment and modalities would allow for simultaneous practice by large groups of male and female athletes or recreational users.
5. Adaptive and rehabilitative facilities should be designed to accommodate the needs of challenged populations.
6. Storage and locker rooms must focus on the needs of staff members and participants. Architects should receive input and direction from those who will be most affected as users or supervisors. Teachers, coaches, and recreation supervisors should research successful new models.
7. Depending on economic resources and local interests, an indoor tennis court, ice rink, or track and field facility might be considered.

Figure 8.1 lists some considerations the planning committee and the institution's architectural consultant should review regarding the amount of space needed for various activities.

You may also want to consider the needs of specialized activities such as curling, gymnastics, resistive strength training, and dance. Figure 8.2 outlines space considerations for these facilities.

Indoor Competitive Playing Spaces

Sport	Playing area in feet	Safety spaces in feet	Total area in feet
Badminton	44 × 20	6 side 10 end	56 × 40
Basketball	50 × 94	10 side 12 end	70 × 118
Handball	46 × 23	No	50 × 25
Hockey	200 × 85	No	200 × 85
Tennis	18 × 40	6 side 10 end	30 × 60
Volleyball	30 × 60	10 side 10 end	50 × 80
Wrestling	24 × 24	10 side 10 end	40 × 40

Minimum ceiling height = 30 feet

Figure 8.1 Indoor competitive playing spaces.

Recommended Square Footage for Multipurpose or Special-Purpose Gyms

Sport	Length × width in feet	Ceiling height in feet
Curling	128 × 14	24
Gymnastics	150 × 100	30
Resistive strength	60 × 60	24
Dance	60 × 60	24

Figure 8.2 Recommended square footage for multipurpose or special-purpose gyms.

Determining Instructional Space Needs

Minimum number of teaching stations =

$$\frac{\text{Number of students}}{\text{Average number of students per class}} \times \frac{\text{Number of class periods per week}}{\text{Total classes per school per week}}$$

Total activity sites =

Minimum number of teaching stations + Total number of intramural and interscholastic stations

---

Figure 8.3 Determining instructional space needs.

Teaching Stations

The planning committee will need to ascertain the number of teaching stations required for the proposed facility. Figure 8.3 shows a formula for calculating teaching stations based on student enrollment.

REQUEST FOR PROPOSALS: THE BID PROCESS

Universities and school districts are usually required by law to solicit competitive bid proposals for major construction projects. Requests for proposals (RFPs) are public documents and must be made available to any firm that wants to bid. A list of potential bidders may be developed from local and regional telephone books or from directories of professional construction agencies and contractors.

The RFP process typically involves the school's central administration, its legal counsel, and its architectural consultants. It disseminates information efficiently and provides a comprehensive description of the proposal to potential builders. This action avoids costly additions or change orders once the construction project is under way. (After construction has begun, any significant alteration in the original plan may lead to cost overruns, reduced confidence, and mutual distrust.)

Bid Specifications

Bids should be developed by trained professionals in the field of architectural engineering, physical education, recreation, and athletics, with input from the various participants who will use the facilities. Bid specifications should address the following considerations.

Construction Bid Components

Section 1: General Requirements

Allowances

Alternatives

Project coordination

Mechanical and electrical coordination

Cutting and patching

Field engineering

Regulatory requirements

Wage rates and scale

Abbreviations and definitions

Alteration procedures

Project meetings

Submittals

Testing services

Construction facilities and controls

Temporary lighting and power

Temporary water and sanitary facilities

Project identification

Materials and equipment

Starting of mechanical systems

Testing and balancing of air and water systems

Contract closeout

Cleaning

Warranties and bonds

Section 2: Sitework

Selective demolition and alteration

Site preparation

Earthwork

Trenching and backfilling

Asphalt paving

Concrete paving

Sanitary building sewer

Storm sewer

Grasses and lawns

Trees, plants, and shrubs

Section 3: Concrete

Sand mixture

Reinforcement requirements

Stress tolerance

Contract specifications

Section 4: Masonry

Unit masonry systems

Section 5: Metals

Structural steel

Joists

Metal roof deck

Steel framing

Metal framing

Expansion control

Section 6: Wood and Plastic

Rough carpentry

Finish carpentry

Section 7: Thermal and Moisture Protection

Building insulation

Fire stopping

Modified bituminous roofing

Flashing and sheet metal

Roof accessories

Joint sealers

Section 8: Doors and Windows

Standard steel doors and frames

Overhead doors

Special door systems

Aluminum door systems

Finish hardware

Glazing

Section 9: Finishes

Furring and lathing

Plaster

Gypsum wallboard

Ceramic tile

Acoustical ceilings

Wood-strip flooring

Resilient flooring

Carpet

Tile

Painting and finishing

Section 10: Specialties

Chalkboards

Metal toilet partitions

Identifying devices

Metal lockers

Folding partitions

Section 11: Equipment

Scoreboards (fixed and portable)

Public address system

Backstops and backboards

Batting cages and other netting

Tennis nets and posts

Volleyball standards, nets, and judges' stand

Gym dividers

Gym equipment

Media facilities

Scorer/timer/announcer facilities

Section 12: Furnishings

Telescoping bleachers

Portable bleachers

Section 13: Mechanicals

Pipe equipment and duct insulation

Water distribution system

Soil, waste, and vent system

Storm drainage system

Plumbing system and fittings

Drains and cleanouts

Plumbing fixtures

Water piping systems

Heat transfer systems

Coils

Air handling units

Ductwork and accessories

Air distribution systems

Air diffusers, grilles, and registers

Controls and instrumentation

Section 14: Electrical

Lighting and controls

Basic materials and methods

Raceways, fittings, and boxes

Wires and cables

Wiring devices

Hand/hair dryers

Disconnectors and motors

Starters

Panel boards

Equipment connections

Grounding

Fire alarm and detection system

Clock system

Telephone and raceway system

Sound system

Public address system

Scoreboard system

Bid Specifications and Construction Completion Timelines

A timeline for completion of the project and each of its components should be included in the bid. This will assist the corporation or institution in setting priorities for ordering materials; allocating laborers and seeking subcontractors; and acquiring specialized machinery and construction materials. It will also incorporate potential labor contract negotiations and work stoppages into the bid-letting process.

With this same time frame, your legal counsel must ensure that provisions for installment payments have been stipulated contingent on approval by the agency's consultant. The agreement should also specify any payment penalties for unsatisfactory construction or work not completed by the negotiated finish date.

Reviewing the Bid Proposals

Construction proposals should be presented to the senior leadership of the institution by the consultant/architect and representatives of the planning committee. The architect will provide an overview of the concept and proposal and will answer technical questions. Committee members will respond to questions concerning program needs and student or community interests and participation patterns. The audience for this presentation should include members of the school's governing body (board of education, board of regents, executive committee, city council) and community or campus user groups, donor/benefactors, and representatives from media outlets.

Sample Construction Bid Form

Bid Tabulation Form
Jackson Fieldhouse Project
Single Prime Building Contract

	Bidders			
	Company A	Company B	Company C	Company D
Affirmative Action Certified	Yes	Yes	Yes	Yes

Total Bid
    Four 90' × 50' courts
    30-foot ceilings
    Exterior walls
    HVAC
    Electrical
    Plumbing
	$2,236,938	$2,296,421	$2,143,140	$2,315,000

Company change orders	**Company A**	**Company B**	**Company C**	**Company D**
Gymnastics pit	$ 7,441	$ 8,200	$ 8,200	$ 6,500
Steel entry doors	1,417	3,444	2,445	2,656
Fire alarm control panel	11,316	13,112	11,390	11,707

Figure 8.4 Sample construction bid form.

The details of all bid proposals should be presented to an economic and fiscal control subcommittee well before the final presentation date. At this meeting, questions concerning engineering and technical contract provisions can be reviewed in detail by the planning committee, the institution's engineering consultant, the institution's attorney, the construction firm's engineer, and other staff specialists. This subcommittee will recommend acceptance or rejection of each construction proposal to the senior governing board. Final review and approval or rejection will be the responsibility of that board. Figure 8.4 is a sample bid proposal.

The primary purpose of competitive bidding is to attain the lowest cost for those building and/or equipment items specified in the request for proposals. Public institutions are usually required by law to justify their reasons for selecting a bid other than the lowest. Typical reasons for not accepting the lowest bid proposal include the following.

1. The proposal contains alternatives to the equipment specifications.

2. The proposal contains alternatives to the project plans specified.

3. Other agencies that have used the services of the low bidder give it a poor rating.

4. The low bidder cannot meet the required construction timeline.

5. The low bidder cannot provide insurance bonding.

6. The low bidder cannot guarantee that subcontractors will meet equipment and timeline specifications.

LEGAL AND LEGISLATIVE CONSIDERATIONS

The construction proposal must be developed with care to meet the requirements of Title IX, the Americans With Disabilities Act, and various environmental laws. Legal counsel, representatives of women's and men's sport programs, advocates for physically challenged citizens and students, and specialists in environmental protection should be asked to periodically review plan proposals and consider the potential effects of the plan on programming and scheduling capabilities.

SAFETY STANDARDS

To avoid negligence liability in the basic construction of a new or remodeled facility, legal issues, building code requirements, and practical considerations should be researched. The facility must comply with all provisions of the ADA, including the following.

- Adequate lighting
- Barrier-free entries and exits
- Ease of access to seating areas
- Emergency response capability (weather, fire, terrorism, and medical emergencies)
- Barrier-free access to service areas (toilets, concessions, smoking and ticket areas, telephones, and medical facilities)
- Exits near vehicle parking and traffic patterns
- Designated parking spots for physically disabled patrons
- Ease of surveillance and control of spectator behaviors or law violations
- Buffer zones between spectators and playing areas or player entrances
- Accessible drinking fountains, fire alarms, fire extinguishers, and thermostats
- Electrical outlets and motors equipped with ground fault circuit interrupters

PRESENTING THE SELECTED PROPOSAL

A formal meeting should be arranged where senior institution officials, city government leaders, members of the planning committee, and media representatives can be comfortably seated. The agenda should define the program and should be divided into four components:

1. project overview,
2. cost overview,
3. construction specifications, and
4. questions and answers.

Project Overview

Highlighted features should include all innovative and customer-responsive facilities, state-of-the-art equipment, and the multipurpose, quick conversion features of the facility. The architect should begin by presenting a three-dimensional drawing of the building's exterior features and a site plan demonstrating its orientation on the site and its relation to nearby buildings. An overview of the floor plans for all activity spaces and support facilities should follow. A scale model can be helpful to illustrate colors, relative sizes, and relationships to other buildings, parking facilities, outdoor activity sites, and streets or highways.

Cost Overview

A review of firms that submitted bids and the actual bid proposals should come next, along with commentary concerning how closely the successful bidder met the bid specifications. A short summary of relevant factors should follow to present a rationale for selection of the successful construction firm. This procedure is especially important when a construction proposal other than the low bid has been selected.

Construction Specifications

Engineering and construction data should be made available to interested parties but need not be described in detail at this point. Timelines for construction should specify projected dates on which electrical power, water, heat, telephone service, or traffic patterns may be disrupted. A site for storage of construction supplies, earthen materials, and heavy equipment should be designated and defined as off limits to observers and pedestrians. Plans for excavation and removal of underground tanks and toxic earthen materials must also be defined.

A Mixed Bequest

You have been informed by the estate of an alumnus that the property adjacent to the current gymnasium will be given to the school. However, if construction is planned, the school will be required to remove old underground chemical storage tanks and any surrounding contaminated subsoils before beginning any new construction project. What agencies will need to be involved in assessing and monitoring the environmental protection efforts? What complicating factors might be encountered during the removal of tanks and polluted subsoils?

Questions and Answers

Responses to reporters' questions should be brief and accurate and should refer to the program and student needs the original proposal was based on.

CONTRACT PROVISIONS

Once your planning committee and architectural consultant have agreed that the design and bid specifications represent the interests of various user groups, these requirements are stipulated in the contract. Executives of the construction firm and your institution will sign this document and enter into a formal business relationship. Key contract provisions are cited in figure 8.5.

EVALUATING YOUR FACILITY CONSTRUCTION PLAN

In order to justify expenditures to taxpayers and to your administrative leadership, you should conduct

Recommended Construction Contract Provisions

Article 1: General Provisions

   a. Labor and materials
   b. Taxes
   c. Permits, fees, and notices
   d. Construction schedules
   e. Site information

Article 2: Owner rights and responsibilities

Article 3: Contractor rights and responsibilities

Article 4: Administration of the contract

Article 5: Changes in contract provisions

Article 6: Progress and completion

Article 7: Payment schedule

Article 8: Protection of persons and property

Article 9: Insurance and bonds

Article 10: Uncovering and correction of work

Article 11: Miscellaneous provisions

Article 12: Termination or suspension of contract

Figure 8.5 Recommended construction contract provisions.

a construction plan evaluation after the project is finished. This measure may also provide insights concerning any planning flaws that should be corrected before a similar project is initiated by your department or another school or division in your school district. Assessment factors should include the degree to which

1. the project stayed within specified cost guidelines,

2. project specifications were met,

3. instructional program needs were met,

4. recreational program needs were met,

5. athletic program needs were met,

6. intramural program needs were met,

7. nonschool program needs were met, and

8. equipment specifications were met.

Summary

To successfully plan for facilities, you should

1. explore funding sources;

2. decide what personnel should be included in the membership of the project planning team;

3. determine selection criteria for choosing a competent architect/consultant to advise your planning committee;

4. require site selection guidelines include seismic considerations and environmental pollution assessments;

5. require engineering specifications focus on specific program and participant needs;

6. open bidding opportunities to local, regional, or nationwide competition;

7. make sure bid proposal selection criteria have been clearly specified;

8. decide on proposal presentation methods; and

9. develop an evaluation plan to assess all construction planning criteria and procedures.

Chapter 9
Facility Renovation

Facility renovation can be a practical consideration in geographic areas where land is scarce, when a building has been identified as a protected historic site, when alumni attach great sentiment to an existing facility, or when remodeling can address long-range program and customer needs.

Remodeling or renovating an existing sport facility can also provide an economical alternative to the expense of constructing a new physical plant. It allows an institution to preserve the external features of an existing facility while expanding internal components or developing specialized areas that respond to customer needs and interests.

Renovation involves a number of factors, beginning with the initial planning efforts and continuing throughout the entire remodeling process. This chapter will give you guidelines for addressing those factors.

In this chapter, you will learn

1. a rationale for assessing future needs,
2. why needs assessment is important in selecting the types of facility renovations needed,
3. various feasibility considerations that directly relate to renovation projects,
4. reasons to accept or reject the concept of facility renovation, and
5. how to evaluate your renovation plan.

REMODELING: AN ATTRACTIVE ALTERNATIVE

Because of the significant costs associated with property acquisition and new physical plant construction, facility remodeling or renovation can be an attractive, logical alternative. In preparing to make this choice, you and your staff should conduct immediate and long-range assessments to ascertain the needs of all instructional, recreational, athletic, and private-sector programs and customers. You must also consider state and federal equity and inclusion laws and the needs of other potential user groups, such as civic, drama, or music organizations.

Use Form 9.1 (see pages 124-125), Long-Range Program Considerations, to determine and rank order future program needs and emphases. Those needs that are rated high should then be rank ordered by a consensus vote of your staff and submitted to the renovation planning committee for deliberation.

Once you have rank ordered your program and facility needs, you are ready to conduct a cost analysis of each item. This assessment will help you determine whether renovation can be accomplished with annual capital budgeting capabilities or if a public funding referendum is needed.

A Question of Ethics

You have completed the assessment of your long-range program needs and future directions. After the rank ordering procedure, one of your coaches lobbies other staff members to change their vote or to favor his program interests. How will you address this issue? Is this ethical? Should the renovation planning committee be made aware of this independent initiative?

A RENOVATION PLANNING COMMITTEE

As you attempt to achieve maximal customer satisfaction in a facility remodeling project, it is important to draw upon the expertise, knowledge, opinions, and preferences of individuals other than your instructors and activity supervisors. This will lead to a broader base of support as a greater variety of interests and needs are considered and integrated into the remodeling proposal.

To develop a capable and representative renovation planning committee, draw opinions and suggestions concerning facility renovation and equipment innovations from members of various interest groups, including

1. teaching staff,
2. coaching staff,
3. recreation leaders,
4. student leaders,
5. advocates and instructional specialists for disabled people,
6. fitness and conditioning specialists,
7. drama and music representatives,
8. engineers,
9. architects,
10. city government representatives,
11. legal consultants, and
12. the Department of Natural Resources or environmental engineers.

Committee members should be briefed about the prioritized listing of program and facility needs and directed to consult with the members of their departments or other constituents concerning specific program needs, innovations, and sources of information about model facilities.

ASSESSING EXISTING FACILITIES

To determine the extent and type of renovation needed, the renovation planning committee should assess existing facilities. The findings of this study should be contrasted to the physical plant that will best meet the needs of future programs and enrollments. Criteria should include traditions and other historic factors, property needs, construction elements, and program and equipment considerations.

Form 9.2 (see page 126) is a checklist of factors for your renovation planning committee to consider.

FEASIBILITY CONSIDERATIONS

Once you've developed a comprehensive analysis of existing facilities, long-range program needs, and preliminary renovation requirements, then you're ready to conduct a feasibility study to determine how well a remodeled facility will meet immediate and long-range needs. Feasibility studies must consider costs, potential code restrictions, and a range of construction implications that have the potential to disrupt current instructional, recreational, athletic, and academic activities.

The questions in Form 9.3 (see pages 127-129) should be incorporated into your comprehensive feasibility study and answered by members of the renovation planning committee. Interaction among engineers, architects, program specialists, and senior institutional leaders will be needed to integrate construction, program, and funding considerations.

Form 9.4 (see pages 130-131) uses a checklist format to ask questions about instructional, recreational, athletic, conditioning, and private-sector needs. The form will help members of the feasibility assessment or renovation planning committee gather detailed information during the feasibility planning effort.

POLITICAL CONSIDERATIONS

Now that you have identified a wide range of program considerations, user needs, and feasibility issues, it's time to turn your attention to the political aspects, which must also be integrated into the decision-making process. Buildings that have been part of a community landscape for several decades may have developed historic and sentimental value among the local citizenry. Total replacement of these structures may create a public outcry that jeopardizes existing project acceptance and potential funding support. It would be prudent to hold public hearings on this issue and to include local citizen representatives on the renovation planning committee.

If the structure has been placed on a register of historic landmarks, demolition or major remodeling alterations may be prohibited. In a college setting, alumni support may be difficult to acquire if a campus structure with numerous sentimental attachments is targeted for removal to create space for a new facility. In a high school setting, similar sentiments may operate. Retention of certain exterior features of the existing facility has successfully resolved this issue in at least one major urban setting.

When all political factors are considered, carefully planned renovation may become a primary consideration if land for new construction sites is scarce.

ECONOMIC CONSIDERATIONS

Generally, questions about cost-effectiveness will be asked frequently throughout any feasibility study of a renovation proposal. Economic questions that have the greatest potential for public controversy are listed in Form 9.5 (see page 132).

DEVELOPING THE RENOVATION PROPOSAL

If the financial and political issues can be resolved and feasibility questions answered satisfactorily, the planning team should be told to proceed with development of plans that reflect immediate and long-term user interests and program needs. Instructional, recreational, athletic, student, and community representatives should be involved in the same roles as in the construction planning phase discussed in chapter 8. A key difference here is the need to have a construction architect present during concept development to evaluate whether plans and proposals can be retrofitted within the existing facility while being alert to the following issues.

1. Potential environmental damage (adjacent waterways, reservoirs, wetlands, prairies, nature sanctuaries)

2. Cost overruns (unforeseen labor negotiations or cost increases and shortages of construction supplies)

3. Code violations (DILHR, OSHA, state and local building regulations)

4. Liability and insurance issues (protecting passersby and neighbors from injury or illness)

5. Political ramifications (upcoming elections with voter sensitivity to potential tax increases)

Presenting the Renovation Proposal

Now that you have reconciled conceptual and feasibility issues and developed initial renovation plans, you and the members of your planning committee are ready to present your proposal to senior institutional leaders and decision makers. Ideally, this presentation should be made by the renovation committee architect with support from planning committee members, alumni, or community representatives. The renovation proposal components should make the following points.

a. Future and emerging program needs for instructional, athletic, recreational, and other user groups will be better served by the proposal.

b. The essence of the original structure will be retained. This may also be a strategically important time to describe the community and alumni support for this proposal.

c. All feasibility issues have been resolved.

d. Renovation costs will be lower than the costs of site acquisition and new construction.

This approach will present senior leaders with a logical, focused overview of project factors that address program needs, public concerns, and funding issues.

LETTING BIDS

With the support of the institutional leadership, you are ready to solicit competitive bids for the renovation project. Depending on the size of the project, a public notice soliciting bid proposals can be published in local newspapers, in trade journals within a general geographic area, or throughout the nation. The request for proposals should specify the project's size, its location, and the construction time frame.

A renovation project manual that specifies construction details, materials, and requirements should be made available to potential bidders. This manual is assembled by the engineering specialists of the firm awarded the renovation bid in cooperation with the construction engineering consultant selected by your committee. Potential bidders must be told where they can get the bid project manual and what their deadlines are for estimating and submitting projected costs.

Information for Renovation Bidders

For remodeling projects, it may be necessary to provide bidders with copies of bid components.

1. Renovation proposals, including plans and specifications

2. Plans of the existing facility

3. Photographs of the facility and adjacent properties or structures

4. Samples of materials used in construction of the original facility

5. Site survey and subsurface geotechnical information (this will tell bidders from other cities whether they need to lease or rent heavy equipment or subcontract the services of an earth-moving contractor)

Getting What You Pay For

Your request for proposals (RFP) results in four renovation bids. Only one bid falls within your projected renovation budget. It is clear that the low-bid firm has used nonunion subcontractors and has proposed equipment that is allegedly of similar quality but is not the exact equipment specified in your proposal. Can you accept one of the higher bids? What justifications would you use? Who would need to review and approve this action?

EVALUATING YOUR RENOVATION PLAN

You should evaluate your renovation plan after the project is completed. Here are some questions to ask.

1. Was the project completed within budget?

2. Was the final cost less expensive than new construction?

3. Was the project completed within the projected construction time frame?

4. Did the renovation meet program goals?

5. Did the renovation meet square footage needs?

6. Did the renovation meet equipment needs?

Summary

When you are contemplating remodeling or renovating an existing structure as an alternative to new construction,

1. consider long-range program and facility needs;

2. put together a renovation planning committee that reflects potential future user groups;

3. consider various political and historic factors;

4. confirm economic and funding considerations;

5. evaluate whether the renovation proposal achieves architectural compatibility with surrounding facilities; and

6. identify bidding procedures and bid evaluation criteria.

▌Form 9.1 — Long-Range Program Considerations

A. What future emphasis will be given to the following curricular offerings?

	High	Medium	Low
1. Team sports	_____	_____	_____
2. Lifetime, leisure sports	_____	_____	_____
3. Health/fitness-related activities	_____	_____	_____
4. Dance and choreography	_____	_____	_____
5. Adapted instruction	_____	_____	_____

B. What level of customer demand will exist for recreational needs in the following areas?

	High	Medium	Low
1. Competitive sports for adult users	_____	_____	_____
2. Structured intramural activities for college or high school students	_____	_____	_____
3. Unstructured, drop-in activities	_____	_____	_____
4. Specialized activities			
a. conditioning sections	_____	_____	_____
b. aquatic classes	_____	_____	_____
c. racquet sport instruction	_____	_____	_____
5. Adaptive recreational interests and needs	_____	_____	_____

C. What will be the demand for future athletic facilities?

	High	Medium	Low
1. Expanded gym space	_____	_____	_____
2. Expanded locker, shower, toilet, and laundry facilities	_____	_____	_____
3. Expanded rehabilitation and training room facilities	_____	_____	_____
4. Expanded team video and meeting room spaces	_____	_____	_____
5. Expanded resistive strength-training facilities	_____	_____	_____
6. Expanded office spaces (for coaches, counselors, team physicians)	_____	_____	_____
7. Increased spectator seating	_____	_____	_____
8. Improved spectator sight lines	_____	_____	_____

	High	Medium	Low
9. Modern scoreboard/message board	___	___	___
10. Improved public address system	___	___	___
11. Improved ventilation	___	___	___
12. Improved lighting and electrical circuitry	___	___	___
13. Safety code compliances	___	___	___
14. ADA access	___	___	___

D. What will be the intensity of need of other user groups?

	High	Medium	Low
1. Drama, performing arts, or music organizations	___	___	___
2. Community meetings	___	___	___
3. Special Olympics or amateur athletic organizations	___	___	___
4. Youth organizations	___	___	___

▌ Form 9.2 — Assessing Current Facilities

Historic significance	High	Medium	Low
1. What is the degree and intensity of alumni interest?	_____	_____	_____
2. How significant is the facility in the history of the campus or institution?	_____	_____	_____
3. How committed are the alumni to replacing, renovating, or remodeling the existing structure?	_____	_____	_____

Property and land considerations	Yes	No
1. Is the facility listed on a registry of historically protected structures?	_____	_____
2. Is adjacent property available for remodeling or expansion?	_____	_____
3. Is information concerning the weight-bearing capacity of soils available?	_____	_____
4. Is property available for storage of construction soils and heavy equipment?	_____	_____
5. Is property available for parking lots, streets, highways, and access areas?	_____	_____

Construction factors	Yes	No
1. Will code changes be required in the existing or remodeled facility?	_____	_____
2. Can the remodeled structure be matched to the existing architecture?	_____	_____

Program and equipment factors	Low	Medium	High
1. What will be the demand for additional space for various programs?	_____	_____	_____
2. What will be the demand for specialized facilities?	_____	_____	_____
3. To what degree does the existing equipment inventory meet the needs of current programs?	_____	_____	_____
4. To what degree does the current equipment inventory meet the needs of the current customer base?	_____	_____	_____
5. To what degree will the current equipment inventory meet the needs of future programs and user groups?	_____	_____	_____

▌ Form 9.3 — Feasibility Assessment Criteria

1. What is the condition of the existing facility? What is its structural soundness? Will the building withstand remodeling? Renovation? Expansion?

_____

_____

_____

2. Can the existing facility be expanded, adapted, or modified to meet projected needs?

_____

_____

_____

3. Can the existing or expanded facility accept new equipment designed to respond to emerging or future customer needs and interests?

_____

_____

_____

4. Considering all program and customer needs, what is the total square footage requirement? What square footage is available within the existing facility?

_____

_____

_____

5. What ventilation, lighting, and acoustical problems will renovation create? What problems will it resolve?

_____

_____

_____

6. Is adequate property available next to the existing facility? What space requirements between buildings are mandated by local codes? What demolition costs will be incurred in clearing adjacent properties?

_____

_____

_____

7. What are the projected costs for land acquisition, construction, and equipment installation?

_____

_____

_____

8. If vertical expansion is under consideration, what are the load-bearing capacities of the current facility and the soils within any adjacent spaces?

_____

_____

_____

9. What volume of earth will it be necessary to move or store?

_____

_____

_____

10. What impact will remodeling or expansion have on parking? On traffic patterns? On pedestrian thoroughfares?

_____

_____

_____

11. What will be the impact of renovation on the topographic and aesthetic features of the existing facility or area?

_____

_____

_____

12. What will be the effect of renovation on major engineering and utility functions, such as street, highway, sewer, electrical, and gas/electric services?

_____

_____

_____

13. What hazardous materials will be exposed in the existing facility during construction? What management procedures will be required?

_____

_____

_____

14. What are the energy considerations in terms of heat or cooling loss and gain, new equipment, and code compliance?

_____

_____

_____

15. What time frame is projected for renovation? What time pressures exist?

_____

_____

_____

16. What flooring needs must be met? What will happen to the old floor? Will new flooring materials be used?

_____

_____

_____

17. What resources are available to fund the project? What percentage of the funding will be allocated from government support? What percentage from fiscal revenues? What percentage from student fees?

_____

_____

_____

18. What percentage of the required resources must be acquired through fund-raising efforts? What is the potential for funding from various donors, grants, or bequests?

_____

_____

_____

19. What new maintenance and personnel needs will be created by an expanded or renovated facility?

_____

_____

_____

■ Form 9.4 — Assessing Facility Renovation Needs and Feasibility

Instructional needs	Yes	No
1. Will future instruction feature		
team sports?	_____	_____
leisure activities?	_____	_____
racquet sports?	_____	_____
aquatic activities?	_____	_____
2. Will disabled populations be provided instructional services?	_____	_____
3. Will enrollments increase markedly?	_____	_____
4. Will multiple sections be required for any curricular offering?	_____	_____
5. Will rapid conversion be necessary to accommodate athletics and recreation activities?	_____	_____
6. Will recreation activities be offered simultaneously with instructional activities?	_____	_____

Recreational needs	Yes	No
1. Will recreation activities be		
structured?	_____	_____
or unstructured?	_____	_____
2. Will activities emphasize		
team sports?	_____	_____
conditioning activities?	_____	_____
racquet sports?	_____	_____
aquatics?	_____	_____
adapted recreation?	_____	_____
3. Will recreation activities be offered		
throughout the day?	_____	_____
before and after the instructional day?	_____	_____
evenings?	_____	_____
noon hours?	_____	_____

Athletic needs	Yes	No
1. Will there be need for increased numbers of		
gyms?	_____	_____
conditioning facilities?	_____	_____
locker rooms?	_____	_____
team rooms?	_____	_____
equipment inventories?	_____	_____
2. Will additional sports or competitive levels be added?	_____	_____
3. Will athletic and recreational activities be offered simultaneously?	_____	_____

Conditioning needs	Yes	No
1. Will customers want facilities for		
aerobic conditioning?	_____	_____
resistive strength conditioning?	_____	_____
rhythmic conditioning?	_____	_____
2. Will activities emphasize team sports?	_____	_____

Private-sector needs	Yes	No
1. Is there demand for		
community meeting space?	_____	_____
private-sector activity rentals?	_____	_____
2. Will the private-sector demand encroach on prime time athletic practice times?	_____	_____

■ Form 9.5— Potential Economic Controversy

	Yes	No
1. Can remodeling plans be directly associated with assessments of long-term program needs?	___	___
2. Will existing building systems need to be completely replaced in order to be compatible with the new system components of a remodeled section or building addition?	___	___
3. Have accident prevention costs been considered so that user safety will not be jeopardized by attempts to design a larger spectator capacity or increase the number of activity facilities in an existing site?	___	___
4. If increased usage will result from remodeling, will there be costs associated with providing a corresponding number of		
parking spaces?	___	___
storage spaces?	___	___
shower rooms?	___	___
locker rooms and toilet facilities?	___	___
5. Will there be costs associated with highway and street improvements?	___	___
6. Will costs increase because government agencies require additions or modifications in order to achieve code compliance?	___	___
7. Will the remodeled facility add personnel costs in terms of increased supervision and maintenance staff?	___	___

Appendix A

Organizations That Publish Equipment and Facility Standards

Adapted Sport and Competition

American Association of the Deaf
3607 Washington Blvd., Ste. 4
Ogden, UT 84403-1737
801-393-8710
TTY: 801-393-7916

Dwarf Athletic Association of America
418 Willow Way
Lewisville, TX 75067
214-317-8299

National Amputee Golf Association
P.O. Box 1228
Amherst, NH 03031-1228
603-673-1135

National Handicapped Sports
451 Hungerford Dr., Ste. 100
Rockville, MD 20850
301-217-0960

National Wheelchair Basketball Association
Univ. of Kentucky
110 Sector Bldg.
Lexington, KY 40506-0219
606-257-1623

Special Olympics International
1325 G. St. NW, Suite 500
Washington, DC 20005
202-628-3630

United States Association for Blind Athletes
33 N. Institute St.
Colorado Springs, CO 80903
719-630-0422

U.S. Cerebral Palsy Athletic Association
34518 Warren Rd., Suite 264
Westland, MI 48185
313-425-8961

Archery

National Archery Association
One Olympic Plaza
Colorado Springs, CO 80909-5778
719-578-4576

Badminton

United States Badminton Association
One Olympic Plaza
Colorado Springs, CO 80909
719-578-4808

Baseball

American Amateur Baseball Congress
118-19 Redfield Plaza
Marshall, MI 49068
616-781-2002

National Collegiate Athletic Association
6201 College Blvd.
Overland Park, KS 66211-2422
913-339-1906

**National Federation of State
  High School Associations**
11724 NW Plaza Cir.
P.O. Box 20626
Kansas City, MO 64195-0626
816-464-5400

United States Baseball Federation
2160 Greenwood Ave.
Trenton, NJ 08609
609-586-2381

Basketball

National Basketball Association
645 Fifth Ave., 10th Floor
New York, NY 10022
212-826-7000

National Collegiate Athletic Association
6201 College Blvd.
Overland Park, KS 66211-2422
913-339-1906

**National Federation of State
  High School Associations**
11724 NW Plaza Cir.
P.O. Box 20626
Kansas City, MO 64195-0626
816-464-5400

Curling

United States Curling Association
1100 Center Point Dr., P.O. Box 866
Stevens Point, WI 54481
715-344-1199

Field Hockey

U.S. Field Hockey Association
One Olympic Plaza
Colorado Springs, CO 80909
719-578-4567

Fitness and Conditioning

Aerobics and Fitness Association of America
15250 Ventura Blvd., Suite 200
Sherman Oaks, CA 91403
818-905-0040

National Strength and Conditioning Association
500 Communication Circle, Suite 204
Colorado Springs, CO 80905
719-632-6722

**President's Council on Physical Fitness
  and Sports**
701 Pennsylvania Ave. NW, Suite 250
Washington, DC 20004
202-272-3421

U.S. Water Fitness Association
P.O. Box 3279
Boynton Beach, FL 33424
407-732-9908

U.S. Weightlifting Federation
One Olympic Plaza
Colorado Springs, CO 80909
719-578-4508

Football

National Collegiate Athletic Association
6201 College Blvd.
Overland Park, KS 66211-2422
913-339-1906

**National Federation of State
  High School Associations**
11724 NW Plaza Cir.
P.O. Box 20626
Kansas City, MO 64195-0626
816-464-5400

Golf

United States Golf Association
P.O. Box 708
Far Hills, NJ 07931
908-234-2300

Hockey

National Collegiate Athletic Association
6201 College Blvd.
Overland Park, KS 66211-2422
913-339-1906

**National Federation of State
 High School Associations**
11724 NW Plaza Cir.
P.O. Box 20626
Kansas City, MO 64195-0626
816-464-5400

National Hockey League
1800 McGill College Ave., Suite 2600
Montreal, Quebec, Canada H3A 3J6
514-288-9220

Judo

United States Judo Association
19 N. Union Blvd.
Colorado Springs, CO 80909
719-633-7750

Lacrosse

The Lacrosse Foundation
113 W. University Pkwy.
Baltimore, MD 21210
410-235-6882

National Collegiate Athletic Association
6201 College Blvd.
Overland Park, KS 66211-2422
913-339-1906

U.S. Women's Lacrosse Association
P.O. Box 278
Amherst, MA 01004
413-253-0328

Luge

U.S. Luge Association
P.O. Box 651, 35 Church St.
Lake Placid, NY 12946
518-523-2071

Olympic Competition

U.S. Olympic Committee
One Olympic Plaza
Colorado Springs, CO 80909-5760
719-632-5551

Racquetball/Handball

American Amateur Racquet Association
1685 W. Unitah
Colorado Springs, CO 80904-2921
719-635-5396

Rowing (Crew)

National Rowing Foundation
P.O. Box 10
Kent, CT 06757
203-927-3875

Rugby

USA Rugby
3595 E. Fountain Blvd.
Colorado Springs, CO 80910
719-637-1022

Squash

United States Squash Racquets Association
23 Cynwyd Rd., P.O. Box 1216
Bala Cynwyd, PA 19004
215-667-4006

Soccer

American Youth Soccer Organization
5403 W. 138th St.
Hawthorne, CA 90250
310-643-6455

United States Soccer Federation
1801-1811 S. Prairie Ave.
Chicago, IL 60616
312-808-1300

Softball

Amateur Softball Association of America
2801 NE 50th St.
Oklahoma City, OK 73111-7203
405-424-5266

**National Federation of State
High School Associations**
11724 NW Plaza Circle
P.O. Box 20626
Kansas City, MO 64195-0626
816-464-5400

Sports Medicine and Rehabilitation Services

American College of Sports Medicine
P.O. Box 1440
Indianapolis, IN 46206-1440
317-637-9200

**American Orthopedic Society
for Sports Medicine**
6300 N. River Rd., Suite 200
Rosemont, IL 60018
847-292-4900

American Sports Medicine Association
660 W. Duarte Rd.
Arcadia, CA 91007
818-445-1978

National Athletic Trainers Association
2952 Stemmons Fwy., Ste. 200
Dallas, TX 75247-6103
214-637-6282

Swimming and Diving

**National Collegiate Athletic Association
(Rules and Equipment)**
6201 College Blvd.
Overland Park, KS 66211-2422
913-339-1906

**National Spa and Pool Institute
(Pool Dimensions and Equipment)**
2111 Eisenhower Ave.
Alexandria, VA 22314
703-838-0083

Synchronized Swim

United States Synchronized Swimming
Pan American Plaza
201 S. Capitol Ave., Ste. 510
Indianapolis, IN 46225
317-237-5700

Table Tennis

USA Table Tennis Association
One Olympic Plaza
Colorado Springs, CO 80909
719-578-4583

Team Handball

United States Team Handball Federation
1750 E. Boulder St.
Colorado Springs, CO 80909-5768
719-578-4582

Tennis

United States Tennis Association (Rules)
70 W. Red Oak Lane
White Plains, NY 80604
914-696-7000

**United States Tennis Court and Track Builders
Association (Surfaces and Equipment)**
720 Light St.
Baltimore, MD 21230-3816
410-752-3500

Track and Field

National Collegiate Athletic Association
6201 College Blvd.
Overland Park, KS 66211-2422
913-339-1906

**National Federation of State
  High School Associations**
11724 NW Plaza Cir.
P.O. Box 20626
Kansas City, MO 64195-0626
816-464-5400

**United States Tennis Court and Track Builders
  Association (Surfaces and Equipment)**
720 Light St.
Baltimore, MD 21230-3816
410-752-3500

Volleyball

USA Volleyball
3595 E. Fountain Blvd., Ste. I-2
Colorado Springs, CO 80910-1740
719-637-8300
800-275-8782

Water Polo

U.S. Water Polo Inc.
201 S. Capitol Ave., Suite 520
Indianapolis, IN 46225
317-237-5599

Wrestling

National Collegiate Athletic Association
6201 College Blvd.
Overland Park, KS 66211-2422
913-339-1906

**National Federation of State
  High School Associations**
11724 NW Plaza Cir.
P.O. Box 20626
Kansas City, MO 64195-0626
816-464-5400

Appendix B

Resources for Facility and Equipment Management

Association of School Business Officials International
11401 N. Shore Dr.
Reston, VA 22090
703-478-0405

Athletic Equipment Managers Association
6224 Hester Rd.
Oxford, OH 45056
513-523-2362

National Association of Educational Buyers
450 Wireless Blvd.
Hauppauge, NY 11788
516-273-2600

National Athletic Equipment Reconditioners Association
960 N. Forest Rd.
Buffalo, NY 14221
716-634-3396

National School Supply and Equipment Association
8300 Colesville Rd., Suite 250
Silver Spring, MD 20910
301-495-0240

National Sporting Goods Association
Lake Center Plz. Bldg.
1699 Wall St.
Mt. Prospect, IL 60056-5780
847-439-4000

Professional Grounds Management Society
120 Cockeysville Rd., Ste. 104
Hunt Valley, MD 21031
410-584-9754

Sporting Goods Agents Association
P.O. Box 998
Morton Grove, IL 60053
847-296-3670

Sporting Goods Manufacturers Association
200 Castlewood Dr.
North Palm Beach, FL 33408
407-842-4100

Tennis Industry Association
200 Castlewood Dr.
North Palm Beach, FL 33408
407-848-1026

Appendix C

Resources for Planning and Renovating Facilities

The following agencies develop or specify professional standards for agency members and for various products and materials manufactured for construction or renovation projects. Several government agencies also develop and enforce standards for public and private-sector facilities and for the building professions. Planners and developers should also consult with local government agencies and architects in order to incorporate local standards, statutes, codes, and ordinances into the framework of a comprehensive building or renovation plan.

Accessibility

Americans With Disabilities Act
Information Office
U.S. Department of Justice
Civil Rights Division
P.O. Box 66738
Washington, DC 20035
202-514-0301

Association for Safe and Accessible Products
1511 K Street NW, Suite 600
Washington, DC 20005
202-347-8200

Institute for Technology Development
Advanced Living Systems Division
428 N. Lamar Blvd.
Oxford, MS 38655
601-234-0158

Acoustics

Acoustical Society of America
500 Sunnyside Blvd.
Woodbury, NY 11797
516-576-2360

Audio Engineering Society
60 E. 42nd St., Ste. 2520
New York, NY 10017
212-661-8528

National Council of Acoustical Consultants
66 Morris Ave., Ste. 1-A
Springfield, NJ 07081
201-564-5859

Architects

The American Institute of Architects
1735 New York Ave. NW
Washington, DC 20006
202-626-7300

The Society of American Registered Architects
1245 S. Highland Ave.
Lombard, IL 60148
630-932-4622

Builders and Contractors

American Subcontractors Association
1004 Duke St.
Alexandria, VA 22314-3512
703-684-3450

Associated Builders and Contractors Inc.
1300 N. 17th St.
Rosslyn, VA 22209
703-812-2000

Associated General Contractors of America
1957 E St. NW
Washington, DC 20006
202-393-2040

Associated Specialty Contractors
3 Bethesda Metro Center, Ste. 1100
Bethesda, MD 20814-5372
301-657-3110

General Building Contractors Association
36 S. 18th St.
Philadelphia, PA 19103
215-568-7015

International Remodeling Contractors Association
1 Regency Dr., 2nd Floor
Bloomfield, CT 06002
203-242-6823

National Association of Minority Contractors
1333 F St. NW, Ste. 500
Washington, DC 20004
202-347-8259

Building Safety

American Society of Safety Engineers
1800 E. Oakton St.
Des Plaines, IL 60018-2187
847-692-4121

National Safety Council
1121 Spring Lake Dr.
Itasca, IL 60143
630-285-1121

Occupational Safety and Health Administration
200 Constitution Ave.
Washington, DC 20210
202-219-8148

Building Science

American Institute of Architects
Council on Architectural Research
Association of Collegiate Schools of Architecture
1735 New York Ave. NW
Washington, DC 20006
202-626-7300

International Council for Building Research Studies and Documentation
Building and Fire Research Laboratory
National Institute of Standards and Technology
Bldg. 226, Rm. B250
Gaithersburg, MD 20899
301-975-5902

National Institute of Building Sciences
1201 L St. NW, Ste. 400
Washington, DC 20005
202-289-7800

Codes

American Institute of Architects
Building Performance and Regulations Committee
1735 New York Ave. NW
Washington, DC 20006
202-626-7448

Basic Building Codes
Building Officials and Code Administrators International
4051 W. Fossmoor Rd.
Country Club Hills, IL 60478
708-799-2300

**National Conference of States
   on Building Codes and Standards**
505 Huntmar Park Dr., Ste. 210
Herndon, VA 22070
703-437-0100

Uniform Building Codes
International Conference of Building Officials
5360 Workman Mill Rd.
Whittier, CA 90601-2298
310-699-0541

Concrete

American Concrete Institute
22400 W. Seven Mile Rd., P.O. Box 19150
Detroit, MI 48219-0150
313-532-2600

Concrete Reinforcing Steel Institute
933 N. Plum Grove Rd.
Schaumburg, IL 60173
847-517-1200

National Precast Concrete Association
10333 N. Meridan, Ste. 272
Indianapolis, IN 46290-1081
317-571-9500

Wire Reinforcement Institute
203 Loudoun St., SW, 2nd Floor
Leesburg, VA 22075
703-779-2339

Doors and Windows

Door and Hardware Institute
14170 Newbrook Dr.
Chantilly, VA 22021-2223
703-222-2010

Laminators Safety Glass Association
White Lakes Professional Building
3310 SW Harrison St.
Topeka, KS 66611-2279
913-266-7014

National Wood Window and Door Association
1400 E. Touhy Ave., Ste. G-54
Des Plaines, IL 60018
847-299-5200

Steel Door Institute
30200 Detroit Rd.
Cleveland, OH 44145
216-899-0010

Steel Window Institute
c/o Thomas Assocs., Inc.
1300 Sumner Ave.
Cleveland, OH 44115-2851
216-241-7333

Vinyl Window and Door Institute
355 Lexington Ave., 11th Floor
New York, NY 10017
212-351-5400

Educational Facility Planning

American Institute of Architects
Committee on Architecture for Education
1735 New York Ave. NW
Washington, DC 20006
202-626-7589

**Council of Educational Facility Planners,
   International**
8687 E. Via De Ventura, Ste. 311
Scottsdale, AZ 85258-3347
602-948-2337

Electrical

**Illuminating Engineering Society
   of North America**
120 Wall St., 17th Floor
New York, NY 10005-4001
212-248-5000

**International Association
   of Lighting Management Companies**
10 Washington Rd.
Princeton Junction, NJ 08550-1028
609-799-5501

National Electrical Manufacturers Association
1300 North 17th St., Ste. 1847
Rosslyn, VA 22209
703-841-3200

National Fire Protection Association
1 Batterymarch Park
P.O. Box 9101
Quincy, MA 02269-9101
617-770-3000

Underwriters Laboratories
333 Pfingsten Rd.
Northbrook, IL 60062
847-272-8800

Engineering

Association of Energy Engineers
4025 Pleasantdale Rd., Ste. 420
Atlanta, GA 30340
770-447-5083

Institute of Industrial Engineers
25 Technology Park/Atlanta
Norcross, GA 30092
770-449-0460

**National Association
of Black Consulting Engineers**
1979 Beaumont Dr.
Baton Rouge, LA 70806
504-927-7240

National Society of Professional Engineers
1420 King St.
Alexandria, VA 22314
703-684-2800

Environment

American Academy of Environmental Engineers
130 Holiday Ct., Ste. 100
Annapolis, MD 21401
410-266-3311

Environmental Protection Agency
401 M St. SW
Washington, DC 20460
202-260-7751

Environmental Systems Research Institute
380 New York St.
Redlands, CA 92373-8100
714-793-2853

Estimating

American Society of Professional Estimators
11141 Georgia Ave., Ste. 412
Wheaton, MD 20902
301-929-8848

**Professional Construction Estimators
Association of America**
P.O. Box 11626
Charlotte, NC 28220-1626
704-522-6376

Facility Management

**Association of Higher Education Facilities
Officers**
1446 Duke St.
Alexandria, VA 22314
703-684-1446

Finishes

Architectural Spray Coaters Association
230 W. Wells St., Ste. 311
Milwaukee, WI 53203
414-273-3430

**Ceilings and Interior Systems Construction
Association**
579 W. North Ave., Ste. 301
Elmhurst, IL 60126
630-833-1919

Association of the Wall and Ceiling Industries
307 Annandale Rd., Ste. 200
Falls Church, VA 22042-2433
703-534-8300

Forest Products Laboratory
1 Gifford Pinchot Dr.
Madison, WI 53705-2398
608-231-9467

Gypsum Association
810 First St. NE, Ste. 510
Washington, DC 20002
202-289-5440

National Paint and Coatings Association
1500 Rhode Island Ave. NW
Washington, DC 20005
202-462-6272

National Terrazzo and Mosaic Association
3166 Des Plaines Ave., Ste. 121
Des Plaines, IL 60018
847-635-7744

Tile Council of America
P.O. Box 1787
Clemson, SC 29633
803-646-TILE

Wallcovering Association
401 N. Michigan Ave.
Chicago, IL 60611-4267
312-644-6610

Flooring

Maple Flooring Manufacturers Association
60 Revere Dr., Ste. 500
Northbrook, IL 60062
847-480-9138

National Oak Flooring Manufacturers Association
P.O. Box 3009
Memphis, TN 38173-0009
901-526-5016

National Wood Flooring Association
233 Old Meramec Stations Rd.
Manchester, MO 63021-5310
314-391-5161

Resilient Floor Covering Institute
966 Hungerford Dr., Ste. 12-B
Rockville, MD 20850
301-340-8580

Indoor Air Quality

Environmental Protection Agency
401 M Street SW
Washington, DC 20460
202-233-9370

**International Society
of Indoor Air Quality and Climate**
P.O. Box 22038, Sub 32
Ottawa, Ontario, Canada KIV 0W2
616-737-2005

Interior Design

American Society of Interior Designers
608 Massachusetts Ave. NE
Washington, DC 20002
202-546-3480

International Society of Interior Design
433 S. Spring St., Ste. 1014
Los Angeles, CA 90013
213-744-1313

Masonry

Brick Institute of America
11490 Commerce Park Dr.
Reston, VA 22091
703-620-0010

Building Stone Institute
P.O. Box 5047
White Plains, NY 10602-5047
914-232-5725

International Masonry Institute
823 15th St. NW
Washington, DC 20005
202-383-3903

Marble Institute of America
33505 State St.
Farmington, MI 48335
810-476-5558

National Concrete Masonry Association
2302 Horse Pen Rd.
Herndon, VA 22071-3499
703-713-1900

Materials Standards

Air Movement and Control Association
30 W. University Dr.
Arlington Heights, IL 60004-1893
847-394-0150

American National Standards Institute
11 W. 42nd St., 13th Floor
New York, NY 10036
212-642-4900

American Society for Testing and Materials
1916 Race St.
Philadelphia, PA 19103-1187
215-299-5400

Mechanical (includes heating, cooling, and plumbing)

American Society of Heating, Refrigerating and Air Conditioning Engineers
1791 Tullie Circle NE
Atlanta, GA 30329
404-636-8400

American Society of Mechanical Engineers
345 E. 47th St.
New York, NY 10017-2392
212-705-7722

American Society of Plumbing Engineers
3617 Thousand Oaks Blvd., Ste. 210
Westlake Village, CA 91362-3649
805-495-7120

American Society of Sanitary Engineering
P.O. Box 40362
Bay Village, OH 44140
216-835-3040

Institute of Heating and Air Conditioning Industries
606 N. Larchmont Blvd., Ste. 4A
Los Angeles, CA 90004
213-467-1158

National Association of Plumbing, Heating, Cooling Contractors
180 S. Washington St., P.O. Box 6808
Falls Church, VA 22040-6808
703-237-8100

Plumbing Manufacturers Institute
800 Roosevelt Rd., Bldg. C, Ste. 20
Glen Ellyn, IL 60137
630-858-9172

Metals

Aluminum Association
900 19th St. NW, Ste. 300
Washington, DC 20006
202-862-5104

American Institute of Steel Construction
1 E. Wacker Dr., Ste. 3100
Chicago, IL 60601-2001
312-670-2400

American Iron and Steel Institute
1101 17th St. NW
Washington, DC 20036-4700
202-452-7100

Copper Development Association
260 Madison Ave.
New York, NY 10016
212-251-7200

Metal Building Manufacturers Association
c/o Thomas Associates, Inc.
1300 Sumner Ave.
Cleveland, OH 44115-2851
216-241-7333

Metal Lath/Steel Framing
600 Federal St., Ste. 400
Chicago, IL 60605
312-922-6222

Sheet Metal and Air Conditioning Contractors National Association
4201 Lafayette Center Dr.
Chantilly, VA 22021
703-803-2980

Steel Deck Institute
P.O. Box 9506
Canton, OH 44711
216-493-7886

Steel Joist Institute
1205 48th St. N., Ste. A
Myrtle Beach, SC 29577-5424
803-449-0487

Passive Heating and Cooling

American Solar Energy Society
2400 Central Ave., Ste. G-1
Boulder, CO 80301
303-443-3130

Energy Efficient Building Association
2950 Metro Dr., Ste. 108
Minneapolis, MN 55425-1560
612-851-9940

Preservation and Restoration

**Association for Preservation Technology
  International**
P.O. Box 3511
Williamsburg, VA 23187
703-373-1621

**Association of Specialists in Cleaning
  and Restoration**
10830 Annapolis Junction Rd., Ste. 312
Annapolis Junction, MD 20701-1120
301-604-4411

Recreational Facilities

National Recreation and Park Association
2775 S. Quincy St., Ste. 300
Arlington, VA 22206-2204
703-820-4940

Security

American Society for Industrial Security
1655 N. Fort Meyer Dr., Ste. 1200
Arlington, VA 22209
703-522-5800

National Crime Prevention Council
1700 K St. NW, 2nd Floor
Washington, DC 20006-3817
202-466-6272

Seismic Technology

Building Seismic Safety Council
National Institute of Building Sciences
1201 L St. NW
Washington, DC 20005
202-289-7800

Federal Emergency Management Agency
Federal Center Plaza, 500 C St. SW
Washington, DC 20472
202-646-2500

Sitework (including landscape and golf course architecture)

American Planning Association
122 S. Michigan Ave., Ste. 1600
Chicago, IL 60603-9604
312-431-9100

American Society of Civil Engineers
1015 15th St. NW, Ste. 600
Washington, DC 20005
202-789-2200

American Society of Golf Course Architects
221 N. LaSalle St.
Chicago, IL 60601
312-372-7090

American Society of Landscape Architects
4401 Connecticut Ave. NW, 5th Floor
Washington, DC 20008
202-686-2752

Swimming Pools

National Pool and Spa Institute
2111 Eisenhower Ave.
Alexandria, VA 22314
703-838-0083

Thermal and Moisture (including roofing and plastics)

Adhesive and Sealant Council
1627 K St. NW, Ste. 1000
Washington, DC 20006-1707
202-452-1500

Asphalt Roofing Manufacturers Association
6000 Executive Blvd., Ste. 201
Rockville, MD 20852
301-231-9050

Institute of Roofing and Waterproofing
4242 Kirchoff Rd.
Rolling Meadows, IL 60008
847-991-9292

National Roofing Contractors Association
O'Hare International Center
10255 W. Higgins Rd., Ste. 600
Rosemont, IL 60018-5607
847-299-9070

Rubber Manufacturers Association
Roofing Products Division
1400 K St. NW, Ste. 900
Washington, DC 20005
202-682-4800

Society of the Plastics Industry
1275 K St. NW, Ste. 400
Washington, DC 20005
202-371-5200

Transportation

**American Association of State Highway
   and Transportation Officials**
444 N. Capitol St. NW, Ste. 249
Washington, DC 20001
202-624-5800

**American Road and Transportation Builders
   Association**
The ARTBA Building
1010 Massachusetts Ave. NW, 6th Floor
Washington, DC 20001
202-289-4434

Institute of Transportation Engineers
525 School St. SW, Ste. 410
Washington, DC 20024-2797
202-554-8050

Transportation Research Board
2101 Constitution Ave. NW
Washington, DC 20418
202-334-2934

Wood and Plastic

American Lumber Standards Committee
P.O. Box 210
Germantown, MD 20875-0210
301-972-1700

American Plywood Association
P.O. Box 11700
Tacoma, WA 98411
206-565-6600

Cultured Marble Institute
1735 N. Lynn St., Ste. 950
Arlington, VA 22209-2022
703-276-2644

Decorative Laminate Products Association
1899 Preston White Dr.
Reston, VA 22091
703-264-1690

National Forest Products Association
111 19th St. NW, Ste. 800
Washington, DC 20036
202-463-2700

National Hardwood Lumber Association
P.O. Box 34518
Memphis, TN 38184-0518
901-377-1818

National Particleboard Association
18928 Premier Ct.
Gaithersburg, MD 20879
301-670-0604

Plastics Institute of America
277 Fairfield Rd., Ste. 100
Fairfield, NJ 07004-1932
201-808-5950

Federal Laws That Specify Standards

Americans With Disabilities Act

Title IX of the Education Amendments Act of 1972

Rehabilitation Act for All Handicapped Children
(P.L. 94-142)

Federal Agencies That Specify Building and Renovation Standards

Department of Industry Labor and Human
Relations (DILHR)

Occupational Safety Health Act

Justice Department (Americans With Disabilities
Act)

Military Construction Specifications
Superintendent of Documents
U.S. Government Printing Office
Washington, DC 20402

Index*

A

A. D. Software, 48
Accessibility. *See also* Facility use
 gender equity in, 4, 96-97, 114-115
 for populations with special needs,
  11, 19, 30-31, 60, 96, 114-115
 restrictive, 4
 standards for, 139
Accidents, reporting of, 33, 81, 85, **90**
Accountability, 22, 47
Acoustics, standards for, 139
Activity leaders, 15
ADA. *See* Americans With Disabilities
 Act (ADA)
Adaptive physical activity
 site considerations for facilities for,
  109
 standards for sport and competition
  in, 133
Administration (administrators)
 on construction planning commit-
  tees, 106
 philosophy of, 5-10, **7, 9,** 93
 role of, 13-14, 34
AEMA (Athletic Equipment Managers
 Association), 45
Aerobics, maintenance checklist for, **64**
Agencies, federal, 146
American College of Sports Medicine,
 104
American Heart Association, 104
American Medical Association, 104
American Red Cross, 84
Americans With Disabilities Act (ADA),
 19, 30-31, 60, 92, 114-115, 146

B

Archery
 maintenance checklist for, **65**
 standards in, 133
Architects
 on construction planning committees, 106
 hiring of, 106-107
 standards for, 139-140
Assessment. *See* Evaluation
Athletic department representatives, on
 construction planning committees,
 105-106
Athletic Equipment Managers Association (AEMA), 45
Athletic facilities, management of,
 10

Badminton
 maintenance checklist for, **65**
 standards in, 133
Baseball
 maintenance checklist for, **66**
 standards in, 134
Basketball
 equipment assessment form for, 43
  (table)
 maintenance checklist for, **67**
 standards in, 134
Bequests, 104
Bias, of facility and equipment managers, 5, **6**
Bidding
 on construction projects, 111-114
 purchasing by, 44, 45
 on renovation projects, 122

 sample bids, 55, 59, **114**
 timing of, 55
Bowling, maintenance checklist for, **68**
Budget. *See also* Funding; Fund-raising
 cost-effectiveness in, 20
 limitations on, 21
 planning by facility and equipment
  managers, 13
 record-keeping in, 32-33
Builders, standards for, 140
Building codes, standards for, 140-
 141
Building safety, standards for, 140
Building science, standards for, 140
Bulk purchasing, 44, 45

C

Cardiopulmonary resuscitation, 84
Cleaning, of equipment, 50
Clerical workers, 15
Coaches
 planning by, 34
 and repair procedures, 49-50
 role of, 15
 selection of, 84
 supervision of, 84
 teaching duties of, 82-83
 training of, 84
Codes, standards for, 140-141
Collegiate athletic departments
 equipment purchasing in, 44
 equipment storage in, 46
Communication systems, 10
Community programs, support for, 11,
 93-94

*Note: Page numbers in bold refer to forms. Tables are identified parenthetically after the page number. Figures are not indexed separately.

Computers, for equipment inventory and distribution, 47-48

Concrete, standards for, 141

Conditioning
  proper training in, 83
  standards in, 134

Construction projects
  architectural and construction consultants for, 106-107
  bidding on, 111-114
  contracts for, 116
  evaluating plans for, 116
  funding of, 104-105
  legal and legislative considerations for, 114-115
  planning committee for, 105-106
  planning of, 10, 103-117
  proposal selection for, 115-116
  safety in, 115
  site considerations, 108-111
  timing of, 113

Consultants, for construction projects, 106-107

Contractors, standards for, 140

Convertibility, 10

Cooling systems, 10, 144, 145

Costs, fixed, 32

Crew (rowing)
  maintenance checklist for, **69**
  standards in, 135

Cross-country, maintenance checklist for, **68**

Curling, standards in, 134

Customers. *See* Users

D

Dance, maintenance checklist for, **69**

Department of Industry Labor and Human Relations (DILHR) Codes, 30, 146

Direct purchasing, 44

Diving
  maintenance checklist for, **76**
  site considerations for, 109
  standards in, 136

Doors, standards for, 141

Durability, 10

E

Education Amendments Act of 1972, Title IX of, 19, 30, 92, 96, 114-115, 146

Educational facilities. *See* Instructional facilities

Electrical systems, standards for, 141-142

Emergency procedures, 81, 82, 84

Endowments, 104

Energy conservation, 10

Engineering standards, 142

Environmental considerations, standards for, 142, 143

Equal access policies, 4

Equipment
  accessing need for, 17-23, **24-28**, 42-43, **52**
  capital (permanent), 20, **28**, 47
  distribution of, 47-49, 81
  evaluating management plan for, 50-51
  expendable, 20, **27**
  fitting of, 47
  funding of, 5, 22-23
  inspection of, 83, 84-85, **89**
  inventory of, 33, 42, 43-44
  maintenance of, 34-35, **38**, 49-50
  management of. *See* Equipment managers; Facility and equipment managers
  management plan for, 41-51, **52**
  marking (identification codes) of, 47
  master roster of, 47, 48
  players' custody of, 47, 48
  policies governing acquisition of, 4-5
  purchasing of, 42-45, 50-51
  replacement plans for, 33, 42
  setting up of, 82
  sharing of, 20, **27, 28**
  storage of, 46-47

Equipment managers, role of, 15

Estimating, standards for, 142

Evaluation
  of equipment management plans, 50-51
  by facility and equipment managers, 13
  of facility construction plans, 116
  of facility maintenance plans, 60, **64**
  planning for, 34-35, **37, 38**
  of renovation plans, 122-123
  of scheduling plans, 97-98
  of supervision plans, 85
  timing of, 34-35, **37, 38**

Exits, 10

Expansion. *See* Construction projects; Renovation projects

F

Facilities
  accessing needs of, 17-23, **24-28**
  assessing need for renovation of, 120, **126**
  construction of, 10, 103-117
  extramural, 80, **87,** 97
  funding of, 10, 22
  identifying responsibility for, 92
  inspection of, 60, **62,** 83, 84-85, **89**
  maintenance of, 34, **37,** 53-61, **62-78**
  management of. *See* Facility and equipment managers
  preparation of, 19-20, 60, **62, 63**
  renovation of, 10, 119-123, **124-132**
  rental of, 94-96, 97, **102**
  requests for, 92, 94-96, **99, 100**
  scheduling of, 91-98, **99-102**
  site considerations for, 108-111
  size of, 32
  supervision of, 79-86, **87-90**

Facility and equipment management plan. *See* Management planning

Facility and equipment managers
  budget planning by, 13
  establishing goals and objectives by, 15-16, 21-22
  evaluation by, 13
  general role of, 3-16
  maintenance procedures established by, 13
  personal philosophy of, 4-5, **6,** 8-10, **9**
  program implementation by, 13
  responsibilities of, 80
  scheduling by, 11-13
  standards for, 142
  use policies established by, 13

Facility design
  guiding principles of, 10
  standards for, 143

Facility use. *See also* Accessibility; Users
  establishing priorities for, 8 (table), 91-92
  permits for, 96, **101**
  personal philosophy of, 4-5
  policies established for, 13

Fencing, maintenance checklist for, **70**

Field hockey, standards in, 134

Finishes, standards for, 142-143

First aid, 81, 82, 84

Fitness and conditioning, standards in, 134

Flexibility, 10
Flooring, standards for, 143
Food preparation areas, 10
Football
    equipment storage checklist for, 42
    maintenance checklist for, **71**
    standards in, 134
Funding. *See also* Budget; Fund-raising
    of construction projects, 104-105
    of equipment acquisition, 5, 22-23
    of facilities, 10, 22
Fund-raising. *See also* Budget; Funding
    resources for, 21-23, 104
    support for, 104-105

G

Gender equity, 4, 96-97. *See also* Title
    IX, Education Amendments Act
    of 1972
Golf
    maintenance checklist for, **72**
    standards in, 135
Golf course architecture, standards for,
    145
Grants, 32, 104
Gymnastics
    maintenance checklist for, **72**
    site considerations for, 109
    supervision of, 80, 82, 83

H

Hallways, 10
Handball. *See also* Team handball
    maintenance checklist for, **73**
    standards in, 135
Heating systems, 10, 144, 145
Helmets, reconditioning and recertifi-
    cation of, 43, 47
High school athletic departments
    equipment purchasing in, 44
    record-keeping in, 48
Historic landmarks, renovation of, 121
Hockey
    maintenance checklist for, **73**
    standards in, 135
    supervision of, 80, 82

I

Ice hockey. *See* Hockey
Ice rinks, site considerations for, 109
Indoor air quality, standards for, 143
Industry grants, 104
Information providers, 31

Injuries, prevention of, 79, 83-84. *See
    also* Safety
Inspection
    of equipment, 83, 84-85, **89**
    of facilities, 60, **62,** 83, 84-85, **89**
Institution
    accessing needs of, 17-18
    philosophy of, 5-10, **7, 9,** 93
    role of, 13-14, 34
Instructional facilities
    management of, 10
    scheduling priorities for, 11-13, 93-
        94
    site considerations for, 111
    standards for, 141
Instructors
    on construction planning commit-
        tees, 105
    planning by, 34
    responsibilities of, 55
    role of, 15
    selection of, 84
    supervision of, 84
    training of, 84
Insurance, 95-96
Interagency planning and cooperation,
    10, 54, 80
Interior design
    guiding principles of, 10
    standards for, 143
Inventory, of equipment, 33, 42, 43-44

J

Judo, standards in, 135

L

Lacrosse, standards in, 135
Landscaping, standards for, 145
Legal counsel, on construction planning
    committees, 106
Legislation, federal, 146
Liability, for negligence, 14, 31, 47, 81
Lighting systems, 10
Locker rooms
    security of, 80
    site considerations for, 109
Luge, standards in, 135

M

Maintenance
    of equipment, 34-35, **38,** 49-50
    establishing procedures for, 13
    evaluating need for, 34-35, **37, 38**
    of facilities, 34, **37,** 53-61, **62-78**

planning for, 10, 33
    requests for, 60, **63**
    responsibility for, 54, 55, 56 (table),
        58 (table)
    timing of, 50, 54-55, 57 (table), 59
Management planning
    for equipment, 41-51, **52**
    evaluation in, 34-35, **37, 38,** 50-51
    legal considerations in, 29-31
    for maintenance of facilities, 53-61,
        62-78
    record-keeping in, 32-33, 48-49
    resources for, 138
    responsibilities for, 34, **36**
    for scheduling, 91-98, **99-102**
    standards for, 142
    for supervision of facilities, 79-86,
        87-90
*Managing, Promoting, and Marketing
    Interscholastic Athletics* (National
    Interscholastic Athletic Adminis-
    trators Association), 22
Masonry, standards for, 143
Materials standards, 143-144
Mechanical systems, standards for, 144
Media
    facilities for, 60
    refreshments for, 60
Medical procedures, 81, 84, 85, **90**
Metals, standards for, 144
Military construction, specifications
    for, 146
Moisture systems, standards for, 145-
    146
Multiprogram use policies, 4, 10
Municipal (construction) bonds, 104

N

National Collegiate Athletic Associa-
    tion (NCAA) regulations, 96
National Committee on Safety of Ath-
    letic Equipment (NOCSAE), 43, 48
National Interscholastic Athletic Ad-
    ministrators Association, 22
Negligence, 14, 31, 47, 81
NCAA (National Collegiate Athletic
    Association) regulations, 96
NOCSAE (National Committee on
    Safety of Athletic Equipment), 43,
    48

O

Occupational Safety and Health Admin-
    istration (OSHA) regulations, 30

Olympic competition, standards in, 135
Organization
    accessing needs of, 17-18
    philosophy of, 5-10, **7, 9,** 93
    role of, 13-14, 34
OSHA (Occupational Safety and Health
    Administration) regulations, 30

P

Parking lots, 10
Participant fees. *See* User fees
Participants. *See* Users
Participation statistics, 32
Passages, 10
Passive heating and cooling systems,
    145
Personnel. *See* Activity leaders; Clerical
    workers; Coaches; Equipment
    managers; Facility and equipment
    managers; Instructors; Supervi-
    sors; Trainers
Planning, as a legal duty, 82. *See also*
    Management planning
Plastics, standards for, 145-146, 146
Players, custody of equipment by, 47,
    48
Plumbing, standards for, 144
Practices, supervision of, 83
Preservation, standards for, 145
Private industry grants, 104
Programs
    goals and objectives of, 15-16
    implemented by facility and equip-
        ment managers, 13
    long-range considerations for, 120,
        124-125
    scope and size of, 18, **24**
    standards and innovations in, 109
    supervision of, 14
Purchase orders, 44
Purchase requisitions, 44, 45, **45**
Purchasing, of equipment, 42-45, 50-51

R

Racquetball
    maintenance checklist for, **73**
    standards in, 135
Record-keeping
    about accidents, 33, 81, 85, **90**
    in budgeting, 32-33
    computers for, 47-48
    in equipment management, 48-49
Records checklist, 33
Recreation Facility Software, 48

Recreational department representa-
    tives, on construction planning
    committees, 106
Recreational facilities
    management of, 10
    scheduling priorities for, 11-13, 93-
        94
    standards for, 145
Refreshments, 60
Rehabilitation Act for All Handicapped
    Children (P.L. 94-142), 146
Rehabilitation services, standards in,
    136
Rehabilitative facilities, site consider-
    ations for, 109
Renovation projects
    assessing existing facilities in, 120,
        126
    assessing feasibility of, 120-121, **127-
        129, 130-131**
    bidding on, 122
    economic considerations of, 121,
        132
    evaluating plans for, 122-123
    planning committee for, 120
    planning of, 10, 119-123, **124-132**
    political considerations of, 121
    proposals for, 121-122
Rental agreement (sample), 97, **102**
Rental fees, 95-96
Repairs. *See* Maintenance
Requests for proposals (RFPs), 107,
    111-114
Research grants, 104
Restoration, standards for, 145
Restrictive access policies, 4
Restrooms, 10
Revenues, 32
RFPs (Requests for proposals), 107,
    111-114
Risk management, 31, 79, 82
Roofing, standards for, 145-146
Rowing (crew)
    maintenance checklist for, **69**
    standards in, 135
Rugby
    maintenance checklist for, **74**
    standards in, 135

S

Safety
    in construction projects, 115
    of environment (facilities), 83
    of equipment, 83

identifying by sport, 18-19
    of individual users, 80, 83
    standards for, 140
    supervisors' training about, 81
Scheduling
    criteria for, 91-92
    evaluating plans for, 97-98
    of evaluation, 34-35, **37, 38**
    of facilities, 91-98, **99-102**
    of maintenance, 50, 54-55, 57
        (table), 59
    resolving conflicts in, 92-93
    responsibility for, 11-13
    by sport, 18-19, 20, 21, **26**
    by sport seasons, 19, **25**
    of supervisors, 82, 83
Scheduling matrix, 92, 93
Security
    of exits, 10
    of personal belongings, 80
    standards for, 145
    of storage areas, 46-47
    when closing facility, 82
Seismic technology, standards for,
    145
Sitework, standards for, 145
Soccer
    maintenance checklist for, **75**
    standards in, 135-136
Softball
    maintenance checklist for, **66**
    standards in, 136
Special needs, accommodating, 11, 19,
    30-31, 60, 96, 114-115
Spectator facilities, 109
Sport seasons
    accessing needs for, 19, **25**
    equipment checks pre- and post-
        season, 49
    purchasing equipment for, 44
    and timing of facility maintenance,
        55, 59
Sports medicine, standards in, 136
Sports programs. *See* Programs
Sports Stats Inc., 48
Squash, standards in, 135
Staff. *See* Activity leaders; Clerical
    workers; Coaches; Equipment
    managers; Facility and equipment
    managers; Instructors; Supervi-
    sors; Trainers
Stairwells, 10
Standards, organizations for, 133-137
Storage, of equipment, 46-47

Storage space
    assessing need for, 46
    determining potential, 46
    records of, 33
    security of, 46-47
    sharing of, 19
    site considerations for, 109
Student representatives, on construction
    planning committees, 106
Supervision
    evaluating plans for, 85
    of facilities, 79-86, **87-90**
    as a legal duty, 82
Supervisors
    identification of, 80-81
    legal duties of, 82-84
    monitoring and evaluating of, 13, 84,
        88
    planning by, 34
    responsibilities of, 55, 80
    scheduling for, 82, 83
    selection of, 84
    supervision of, 84
    teaching duties of, 82-83
    training and qualifications of, 80-81,
        84
    types of, 14
Support facilities, planning, 10
Swimming
    maintenance checklist for, **76**

    site considerations for, 109
    standards in, 136
    supervision of, 80, 82
Swimming pools, standards for, 145
Synchronized swimming, standards in,
    136

T

Table tennis, standards in, 136
Team handball, standards in, 136
Tennis, standards in, 136
Tennis courts, site considerations for,
    109
Thermal systems, standards for, 145-146
Timing
    of bidding, 55
    of construction projects, 113
    of evaluation, 34-35, **37, 38**
    of maintenance, 50, 54-55, 57
        (table), 59
Title IX, Education Amendments Act of
    1972, 19, 30, 92, 96, 114-115, 146.
    See also Gender equity
Track and field
    site considerations for, 109
    standards in, 136-137
    supervision of, 80
Trainers, maintenance checklist for
    supplies for, **76-77**
Transportation, standards for, 146

U

U.S. Centers for Disease Control, 104
Use permits, 96, **101**
User fees, 10, 32
Users. *See also* Facility use
    assessing needs and opinions of, 5,
        10, 32, 34, 85
    proper pairing of, 83
    role of, 15

V

Versatility, 10
Volleyball
    maintenance checklist for, **77**
    standards in, 137

W

Water polo, standards in, 137
Weight training
    site considerations for, 109
    supervision of, 82
Windows, standards for, 141
Wood materials, standards for, 146
Wrestling
    equipment needs for, 21
    equipment repair for, 50
    maintenance checklist for, **78**
    site considerations for, 109
    standards in, 137
    supervision of, 82

About the Author

As the Coordinator of Athletics and Safety for the Madison School District in Madison, Wisconsin, John Olson is responsible for supervising the conduct of 23 sports programs at four different high schools. He works closely with each of the schools' athletic directors to coordinate the efforts of the 300 coaches and 2,000 officials who conduct the district's athletic programs. In addition, he works with the Wisconsin Interscholastic Athletic Association and Southern Wisconsin Athletic Conference on a variety of regulatory and compliance matters. In his role as safety coordinator, Olson collaborates with principals, school safety committees, and law enforcement agencies to enhance security and safety conditions. He is also assistant superintendent of the Madison School District.

Previously, Olson served as a science teacher, coach, athletic director, and assistant principal in Madison schools. He also taught at the University of Wisconsin School of Education from 1980 to 1987. A graduate of the University of Wisconsin at Madison, where he completed his doctorate in educational administration in 1979, Olson is the author of two books on athletic administration and numerous journal articles about athletic and school safety. He is a recipient of the National Federation of State High School Association's Meritorious Service Award and the Wisconsin Athletic Directors' Distinguished Service Award. He is also a member of Wisconsin High School Football Coaches Hall of Fame.

 **American Sport Education Program**

Leader Level

ASEP's Leader Level provides quality resources and courses for coaches and administrators in interscholastic and club sport. In fact, the National Federation of State High School Associations has selected the Leader Level SportCoach Courses as its own coaches education program, called NFICEP–National Federation Interscholastic Coaches Education Program. The Leader Level offers the following:

Leadership Training Seminars

Our Leadership Training Seminars (LTSs) not only show sport administrators how to conduct our courses, they also revitalize them with fresh ideas about how to help coaches be more effective in their coaching roles. Leader Level instructor seminars include

- Coaching Principles,
- Sport First Aid, and
- Drugs and Sport.

Coaches Courses

Once administrators have attended our LTSs, they are prepared to teach our **Coaching Principles Course, Sport First Aid Course,** and **Drugs and Sport Course** to coaches. The courses provide excellent educational opportunities for both new and experienced coaches. At each course, coaches attend a clinic, study the course text and study guide, then take an open-book test.

The Coaching Successfully Series

The books in this series explain how to teach fundamental sports skills and strategies as well as how to build a sports program by applying principles of philosophy, psychology, and teaching and management methods to coaching.

Series Titles
- Coaching Tennis Successfully
- Coaching Swimming Successfully
- Coaching Football Successfully
- Coaching Basketball Successfully
- Coaching Volleyball Successfully
- Coaching Girls' Basketball Successfully
- Coaching Soccer Successfully
- Coaching Baseball Successfully
- Coaching Cheerleading Successfully

SportDirector Series

See facing page for information.

For more information about ASEP and the Leader Level, call toll-free 1-800-747-5698.

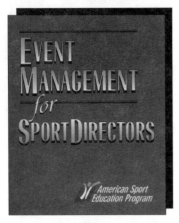

1996 • Spiral • 144 pp • Item ACEP0320
ISBN 0-87322-968-1 • $20.00

Event Management for SportDirectors is a handy tool for planning and managing practically any type or size of athletic event. It provides a comprehensive checklist of 18 categories (along with tasks to be completed for each category), allowing you to conduct even the most complicated functions in a systematic and organized manner.

Whether you're planning a major tournament, managing a fund-raiser, or hosting a small intramural competition, *Event Management for SportDirectors* will guide you each step of the way. This time-saving resource shows you how to plan and manage all of the critical aspects of an event.

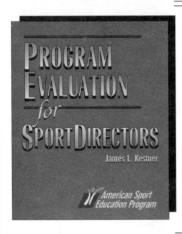

1996 • Paper • 128 pp • Item PKES0505
ISBN 0-88011-505-X • $20.00

Program Evaluation for SportDirectors is a practical, hands-on resource that you can use to evaluate your personnel, facilities and equipment, and program offerings. It contains an easy-to-follow blueprint for conducting evaluations and 20 field-tested forms that can be used or modified to fit your specific evaluation needs.

First, the book explains how to reflect on personal and organizational philosophies, identify who will help in the evaluation process, assess which programs and individuals need to be evaluated, develop an evaluation plan, implement the plan, and review and revise the plan. The heart of the book shows you how to conduct effective personnel evaluations and how to evaluate facilities, equipment, and athletic programs.

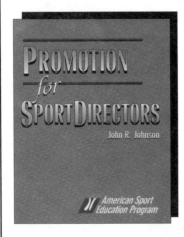

1996 • Paper • 152 pp • Item PJOH0722
ISBN 0-87322-722-0 • $20.00

Promotion for SportDirectors is a cookbook of effective promotional ideas that will get your school lots of attention for very little money. The book gets you started by showing you how to plan for an effective promotional program. You'll discover how your school's philosophy about promotion meshes with your own, how to assess your promotional needs and limitations, and how to develop a comprehensive promotional plan.

This easy-to-use reference also explains each facet of a total promotion plan. You'll learn how to implement a positive public relations program, develop and distribute printed promotions such as programs and schedules, take advantage of radio and television promotion, boost attendance using special promotions, and obtain program sponsorships.

Human Kinetics
The Premier Publisher for Sports & Fitness
http:// www.humankinetics.com /

2335

To place your order,
U.S. customers **call TOLL FREE 1-800-747-4457**.
Customers outside the U.S. place your order using the appropriate telephone number/address shown in the front of this book.

Prices are subject to change.